# Soups and Stews...
## Comfort by the Spoonful

*all you need is a Spoon.*
*Connie Hope*

### Choose a Soup or Stew

### For your lunch or your dinner, but always for a great meal

### Special Section on Crock Pots

Zucchini Fennel Soup

Tomato Basil Soup

White Bean and lime Chicken Soup © Connie Hope

Crock Pot Beef Stew

Beef Stew with variation

Butternut Squash

Printing © in 2016

ISBN 13   978-0-692-64749-3

Printed and bound in China by PRC Book Printing
Jacob D. Hope at Jacob@prcbookprinting.com

This book was created by Connie Hope
Jacket design by Ed Lain, www.LazerGrafixDesign.com.
Production by Andrea Merkert
Illustrations by John W. H. Hope
Photographs by Connie Hope
Edited by Virginia Schuler
Recipe tested and proof read by Hewitt B. McCloskey, Jr.

www.CookingByConnie.com
conniehope4@gmail.com
inadditiontotheentree.blogspot.com
www.thebonnieneuktearoom.com
thebonnieneuktearoom@gmail.com

# Try a Soup or Stew for a
# **Great Meal**
## with your personal
## favorite
## from this
## cookbook.

Here is a key to determine the ease of a recipe for the people who hate to cook and want something easy or the ones who need more of a challenge.

 'Hate to cook' Very Easy , but takes time to cut up veggies

 A little more difficult, has many ingredients, takes time to prepare

 The Chef Extraordinaire—difficult, very few are difficult, but they do take time to prepare

# Table of Contents

## Soups and Stews...
## Comfort by the Spoonful

**By Connie Hope**

# E. Ham

# F. Others—Vegetables, Beans, Cold Soups, Odds and Ends

# V. Stews

# VI. Crock Pot Soups and Stews
## for the Busy Cook

# VII. Soups and Stews with an
## International Flair

Onions © Connie Hope

Garlic © Connie Hope

# Introduction:

Soups or stews are something we all make use of at some time. I know I love a good soup or a hot stew whether it is winter or even in the summer. It can taste just okay if you open a can, or it can taste great if you make it yourself. It is neither difficult, nor time consuming. You can do it. Wouldn't you rather have a great tasting soup or stew? It is the combination of ingredients --meats, veggies, herbs, and spices that create the flavor and cause our palates to water with anticipation. With so many great ingredients at the stores, 'okay' is just not acceptable. This cookbook will help you combine many ingredients to make a great soup or stew to serve for yourself or friends and family. Experiment is the name of the game! Have fun.

I have loved to cook all my life. I can remember standing on a chair with my mother, Blanche, in her kitchen, adding this and that to a can of tomato soup to change the flavor and create my own concoctions. My day was Saturday to cook lunch. So my poor father got to sample all my concoctions. Some were great, and some needed help. But that is how I learned to put different veggies and herbs and spices in soups and stews. After many years of doing this for my friends and family, I decided to pass some of my recipes and ideas on to you.

Today, you can put a soup or stew on for the day either in a crock pot or on the stove in a soup pot. The crock pot is great if you are going to be away from your kitchen and want the soup or stew to be ready for a specific time. I have a tendency to use the old soup pot on the stove, but any of these recipes can be put in a crock pot and cooked all day.

I have created, collected, and improved on these recipes throughout my life. Wherever I have lived, visited or traveled, I have collected recipes from that region. I have lived in St Thomas, and traveled to many islands in the British Virgins, the Windward Island, to Europe, and some just from next door. I have used them, added to them, and sometimes just left them alone.

I hope you enjoy reading and trying all the recipes. These are just some of the great ones.

Connie Hope

# History --Soup 101

'To make a good soup, the pot must only simmer, or 'smile'.
French Proverb

The word soup was borrowed from the French word 'soupe' or 'sop'. The underlying meaning of the word 'soup' is a soaking up of liquid. It was comprised of a bread and a liquid. The bread, which was at the bottom of the bowl, was an important part because it would 'soak' up the liquid. The bread was in effect an alternative way to eat the liquid (at that time, spoons were not used for sop).

The cooking art of combine ingredients in a large pot to make a hot and simply meal is as old as the cooking term itself. Soups have evolved to many areas over the years according to local tastes and availability of ingredients. It was a first course to some, but a meal for the poorer people. Today soups are taken to a new availability, which include, canned, dehydrated, microwavable and portable types of soup. Just to know that dehydrated soups go back as far as the 1800's to supply homes, cowboys, chuck wagons and the military.

In American, the first colonial cookbook, (according to the internet) was published by William Parks in Williamsburg, Virginia in 1742 and included several recipes for soups and bisque. In 1772, The Frugal Housewife, containing an entire chapter on soup was written.

At first English cooking dominated the early colonial cooking, but as new immigrants arrived from different countries, other national soups gained popularity and were adopted. An example was from a German immigrants living in Pennsylvania who brought with them their famous 'Potato soup'.

There are thick soups such as bouillabaisse that nearly cross the line from soup to stew, thin clear consommés, and everything in between. Nearly all cultures have their own specialties. Soups that are popular all over the world are Italian minestrone, French onion, Spanish gazpacho, Chinese Won Ton and Russian Borscht and American New England Clam chowder. They differ in flavor and style, but all are famous.

---

For centuries the food served at the beginning and at the end of a meal stood for the entire thing. The express was 'from eggs to apples' or 'from pottage to cheese'.

In the US during 20th century the expression or idiom became 'From Soup to Nuts' It means 'from the beginning to the end.' A full course dinner would start with the soup and end with a dessert or nuts.

'Soup's on' was in a popular comic strip saying in the 'The Gumps' during 1928. The phase is a call to say that the dinner is on the table. This phase is used many times in today's world.

Information taken from
Wikipedia on the Internet

Check out Andrew F. Smith's book, Souper Tomato which tracks the origin and evolution of Tomato Soup.

# History of Soup 101 (continued)

There are two more words that need to be defined under the topic of soup—chowder and bisque.

Chowder is in the soup family, but is usually thicker and is creamy. Soups are usually made with broth or water base and are much thinner. Chowders are made with a milk base and chocked full of all kinds of ingredients usually including seafood, vegetables and cream. Today there are many different flavors and texture to this soup. One of the most popular chowders is clam chowder. There are two very popular types: New England Clam chowder, which is a cream base. The second is Manhattan Clam Chowder which is a tomato base. Both are very hearty and delicious to warm the palate.

Now to confuse you even more, here is an example. Oyster stew should really be called oyster chowder as it is milk based and not as thick as a stew. Go figure! We're not changing it now.

In the earlier days, seaport towns would put some of their catches in a large pot and boil different types of fish with vegetables and potatoes—fish chowder.

A bisque is a usually a shellfish or fish with cream or milk based soup, but today it is not necessarily only the fish base. Bisque differs from chowder or a stew in that bisque is smooth and usually strained or pureed in a food processor to give it a smooth consistency. Or use an immersion blender. Bisque is a rich, thick and creamy in texture soup. Bisque was first found in France, but today is found all over the world. Generally bisque is made from a highly concentrated stock and is very rich in flavor. (All cream soups are ruined by boiling, so you need to cook them slowly) Such examples are lobster bisque, crab bisque and shrimp bisque, whereas chowder will contain diced vegetables as well as chunks of meat or seafood.

Corn Chowder

*Chowders can also be made with vegetables and meats, such as corn chowder or sausage bean chowder.*

Tomato Bisque with Basil

13

©Connie Hope

# History--Soup 101 (continued)

Here is a list of some of the Traditional regional soups. There are many, many more. I have only listed some of the most popular. Just for your reference.

**Bisque** — A thick, creamy, highly seasoned soup, originally of pureed fish.

**Borscht** — A beet-vegetable soup originally from Ukraine and Russia.

**Bouillabaisse** — is a French seafood stew made with fish, shellfish, onions, tomatoes, white wine, garlic olive oil, saffron and herbs.

**Bouillon** — is a broth made from cooking vegetables, poultry, meat or fish in water.

**Broth** — This refers to the liquid which meat or chicken has been cooked in. Broth occurs as a position between stock and soup. A broth can be eaten as is, where as a stock ( ie. chicken stock) is an ingredient in something more complex. A soup would be more finished than broth. The proverb 'Too many cooks spoil the broth' is first recorded in St Balthazar.

**Consommé** — clarified meat or fish broth. This is a clear soup from France. It is a broth (bouillon).

**Cock-a-leekie** — Leek and potato soup made with chicken stock. It originates from Scotland.

**Clam chowder** — Two major types, New England Clam Chowder made with potatoes and cream, and Manhattan Clam Chowder made with a tomato base.

**Egg drop soup**—a savory Chinese soup made from cracking eggs into boiling water or broth.

**Goulash**—A Hungarian soup of beef, paprika and onions.

# History--Soup 101 (continued)

**Gumbo**—A traditional Creole soup from the American South. It is thickened with okra pods.

**Lentil soup**—A soup popular in the Middle East and Mediterranean.

**Minestrone**—An Italian vegetable soup.

**Miso**—Japanese miso is an example of a concentrated soup paste.

**Scotch broth**—a Scottish soup made with lamb or mutton, barley and various vegetables.

**Stock**—a strained liquid that is the result of cooking vegetables, meat, or fish with other seasonings in water.

They are the juices of the meat, fish or vegetables that are extracted by long and gentle simmering. The bones and caresses can be used to richen the stock. It is a thin clear soup based on stock (or the meat, chicken, or fish used) to which rice, parsley, meat or vegetable may be added. It draws the goodness out of the material and into the liquid or stock.

**Vichyssoise--**A French style soup invented by a French chef at the Ritz Hotel in NYC; French cold puree soup with potatoes, leeks and cream.

America Heritage Dictionary

Wikipidia
The Free Encylcopedia.

An A to Z for Food and Drink, John Axto
Oxford University Press, Oxford 2002, page 44.

# Stock and Broth 101

What is the difference between stock and broth? And bouillon and consommé? The answer is it depends on where you look. If you look in an older dictionary or older cookbook, you get one definition, or in a new dictionary or new cookbook, you get another. Many recipes use them interchangeably.

One school of thought is the difference is in the salt. Stock contains no salt and little seasoning. Broth is seasoned and contains some salt, and bouillon contains a great deal of salt. (Although today, you can purchase a low-sodium version of both broth and bouillon.) Most of my recipes for either have herbs and seasonings in them.

The second difference is stock is never served by itself, but broth can be served by itself as can bouillon and consommé.

The third difference is stock must contain bones in addition to any meat and seasoning. Broth is made from meat and seasoning without the bones. But this can be interchangeable also.

The stock is a liquid extracted from food (meat, poultry, fish, vegetables) slowly cooked in water (or wine) and used in the creating of soups and sauces. Broth is an English term for liquid extracted from meat cooked slowly with water, which is reduced to more like a concentrate and used in soups or as a simple soup by itself. Consommé is a double-strength stock and has been clarified (boiled down, to a concentrated flavoring).

In today's cooking vocabulary, stock usually refers to what we make at home. Broth usually refers to a canned or boxed product you buy. Bouillon usually refers to the powder, paste or little concentrated cubes you buy. Today the terms broth and stock seem to be interchangeable. Both are defined on the web as a flavorful liquid made by gently cooking meat, poultry, seafood or vegetables sometimes with herbs in water.

Whatever the difference, both are something you should keep in your cabinets. I will give you recipes for main types of stocks. Even if you usually buy them, it is interesting to try your hand at them once. You might get hooked.

There are 4 main types of stock—poultry, meat, fish, and vegetable, All four mean the rich savory, liquid created by simmering their ingredients and seasonings in water. The four stocks can be made by using leftovers or items that you might otherwise throw away. You can feel you are being thrifty and not wasteful.

I keep small containers of stock in my freezer and often put the liquid in ice cube trays, freeze them and pop them out into a freezer plastic sealed bag to store. They are perfectly measured amounts for a soup, a sauce, or anything you are making.

# Poultry Stock (Chicken or Turkey)

Poultry stock is a great way to use leftover bones and pieces from de-boning a chicken breast or after you have eaten that bought chicken/turkey roaster. Instead of throwing the bones away, put them in the soup pot add water to cover the bones. You can also add vegetables to your poultry stock. You don't need to use a whole turkey or chicken; you can use leftovers as you did in the vegetable stock. To make the stock darker and rich, roast the bone and vegetable in the oven at 450 degrees for forty to fifty minutes before you put them in your soup pot.

**Put the following items in a stock pot:**
**5 plus pounds chicken or turkey parts or bones**
**1 large onion, chopped**
**3 large carrots, chopped**
**4-5 stalks celery (use the leafy parts as well,**
**they are great in your stock)**
**7-9 cloves of garlic, chopped**
**1 Tablespoon peppercorns**

Simmer for about two hours. If foam forms on the surface, skim it off. Strain the liquid and cool in the refrigerator. The fat will congeal and you can skim it off easily. Same as with the vegetable stock, you can freeze and/ or put the stock into ice cube trays and then in freezer plastic bags.

Chicken Stock © Connie Hope

* boiling stock can cause it to become cloudy.

I get the Costco roasted chicken. We eat some for dinner one or two nights, then I make Chicken stock from the bones and a little of the chicken left on the bones. Then I can make my Lime Chicken and Bean soup.

Any kind of meat can be used: veal, beef, lamb, pork or ham, (you can also try venison, but it will make the stock stronger to the taste)

\* boiling stock can cause it to become cloudy.

# Meat (Beef) Stock

The meat stock is always better if it is dark and rich. Roast your meat, bones and vegetable for forty to fifty minutes at 450 degrees. Then add to your stock pot with water to cover the items. Not roasting the items tends to have the stock lighter in color and not as rich in flavor. Again, you can use whole vegetables or scraps and pieces.

Put the following in a stock ( or soup) pot:

**6-8 pounds lean meat and bones (if more meat is used 6 pounds is fine, if more bones are used 8 pounds is better)**
**3-4 large carrots, chopped (can use pieces)**
**2 large onions, chopped**
**4-5 stalks celery, (you can use the leaves)**
**6-8 cloves of garlic, chopped**
**3-4 bay leaves**
**1 Tablespoon peppercorns**
**½ cup parsley, chopped (fresh is best)**
**Herbs—1 Tablespoon if desired: oregano, basil, thyme**
**Add enough water to cover the ingredients**

Bring just to a boil\*, then immediately lower heat and simmer for about 4 hours. Add more water as needed to keep meat covered.
Strain out solid ingredients and refrigerate stock for several hours.
The fat will be at the top and you can skim it off.

Meat Stock © Connie Hope

# Fish or Seafood Stock

You can use this making fish soup or fish stew, or add to a recipe instead of the liquid listed.
Use a white fish such as haddock or cod, the bones and trimmings. You can also use shells from crab, shrimp or lobster to enrich the stock.

**Put the following in a stock pot:**
**4-5 pounds mild white fish, bones, trimmings or shells of crab, lobster, shrimp**
**2 Tablespoon butter or margarine**
**2 large onions, chopped**
**5 cloves garlic, chopped**
**1-2 stalks celery, (use the leaves also)**
**1 Tablespoon lemon juice (fresh is best)**
**½ cup parsley, chopped (fresh is best)**
**1 teaspoon peppercorn (or use less; you don't want to**
   **overpower the fish stock)**
**1 cup white, dry wine (optional)**
**Enough water to cover ingredient (approximately 3 quarts)**

Melt butter in stock pot and sauté onions, celery, garlic until soft
   about 5-8 minutes.
Add remaining ingredients and simmer slowly for 1 hour. If foam forms, skim off. Cool and strain. As with other stock, you can freeze
   and put into ice cube trays and return to the freezer.

# Vegetable Stock

Making a vegetable stock is a great way to clean out the 'veggie bin' of your refrigerator. Or you can save the trimming of carrots, celery and other vegetables and put them in the freezer in a plastic bag or cut them up from whatever you were making. (I usually stay away from cabbage, broccoli, cauliflower, and asparagus as they can overpower the stock taste.) You will strain your stock so parts and pieces can work. Some examples of great vegetables to use are: mushrooms, peas, corn (or corn on the cob), carrots, squash, sweet potatoes, potatoes, garlic, onions, bell peppers, scallions, green onions, shallots, leeks, beets, green beans, parsley, basil and herbs.

Rule of thumb is half water to half vegetables. Cover the vegetables with water and bring just to a boil*, then immediately lower the heat and simmer for an hour or so. You can add some bay leaves and/or peppercorns for additional  flavor. After an hour, cool the stock, then strain it to remove the pieces of vegetable.

Congratulations, you have just made your first vegetable stock. Now wasn't that easy?

Now that you have read the procedure for making a stock, you can either make it yourself or better yet, buy it at the market. In today's busy world, it is easy to just buy a can or box of stock or broth at the grocery store. We are all busy and don't always have that extra time. But now you'll at least know how to make the stock or broth.

## How do you 'Clarify' the Stock?

Place the stock in a container and refrigerate it overnight or at least for 4-5 hours.
Using a large spoon, skim the excess fat from the top and discard. Separate 2-3 eggs and just use the whites. You can save the yolks for other things. Use a wire whisk to foam the whites of the egg. Pour the foamy egg white into the stock and simmer in large pot. Stir continually. Egg white will rise to surface. Bring to a boil and then lower and simmer unstirred for 30 minutes. The egg whites will trap fine particles from the stock. Place a cheese cloth in a colander and strain the stock. This will remove the particles and the egg white. This will make the stock clean—no particles or bones or pieces of meat.

## The Bouillon Cube

A bouillon cube (used in the US) or a stock cube (used in the UK and Australia) is dehydrated broth. It is made by dehydrating vegetable, meat or chicken stock. It is shaped into a cube or in graduals. The salt content is quite high in a dehydrated cube.

Bouillon cubes are convenient for size to store and inexpensive. The cubes are widely used to flavor soups, stews and casseroles. They may be substituted in a recipe when it states broth or bouillon. Put 1 cup water in a measuring cup and one cube and heat in microwave stirring occasionally. Do this for each cup of bouillon specified in recipe. I, myself, prefer the bones or broth as there is less salt . Some of the most common brands are Maggi, Knorr, Oxo, Herb-ox, Wyler's, Goya, and Kalto and there are many others.

*Boiling stock for too long can cause it to be cloudy.

# Soup and Stew—What's the difference?

Soup is usually meat or vegetables that are cooked in a liquid. Many soups have a meat broth, vegetable broth, milk based or water based broth, but they have lots of liquid. They are served in a bowl and can be either hot or cold.

Stews generally have a much thicker consistency. They are thickened with potatoes, flour, cornstarch, barley, and the liquid is usually called gravy rather than a broth. This mixture is usually chunkier than a soup and is always served hot. There is a minimal amount of liquid in a stew. They are for a hearty appetite. The stew is usually cooked at a much lower temperature; it is not boiled. Stews are cooked for a longer period of time, but much slower. Stews are usually made with either water or broth, but can also be made with beer or exotic juices. The tastes of various ingredients often blend better because of this slower cooking.

If you eat it with a spoon, it is a soup. If you can eat it with a fork, (even if you like using a spoon) it is a stew.

# What do you use to thicken soups or stews?

Here are several methods of thickening soups or stews:
1. Remove some of the cooked vegetables and puree in the food processor or immersion blender. Then return the pureed mixture back to the pot and reheat.
2. White sauce or paste—4-5 Tablespoons flour, add water very slowly and wire whisk in the same direction. Then add to soup mix using the same method.
3. Cornstarch—I part cornstarch, 2 parts water. Add water to cornstarch using a wire whisk and in one direction. Then add the mixture to the soup or stew slowly.
4. White sauce with butter—3 Tablespoons butter, 3 Tablespoons flour, 1 cup water or milk. Slowly melt butter and slowly wire whisk in the flour and slowly whisk in the water or milk. Do not change directions of whisking. Then slowly add to the soup or stew.
5. Barley, rice, noodles or potatoes cut in small pieces will thicken a soup or stew.
6. Instant mash potatoes will also thicken soup or stews. You don't want to use too much, but a $\frac{1}{4}$ or $\frac{1}{2}$ of cup instant potatoes will do a great job.

Vegetables are added in reverse order of the length of time they take to cook. Carrots, potatoes, and turnips are added first as they take the longest. Then the onions, celery, herbs and certain vegetables, rice or pasta are added which don't take as long to cook.

Removing fat from soup
1. Chill the soup over night. The fat rises to the top and will solidify when cold. Then just take a large spoon and skim to remove
2. Float a paper towel on the surface of the soup. It will absorb a lot of the fat, then just discard the paper towel.
3. Float celery leaves on the soup. The fat will stick to them and then can be discarded.

My soup is just chicken and easy to make. But it is a two day process if you want the broth to be rich and delicious.

Here are the things about chicken soup:

I usually buy a roasted chicken at the market. Eat half of it and make soup from the other half.

You can always buy an uncooked chicken and cook it yourself. You'd wanted to cook it at least 2 hours long.

I like to use the already skinned little carrots. Less work.

I always keep a plastic container in my freezer for leftover veggies from meals. Then when I make soup, I just put them in for flavor. I also save the juice from the veggies cans for the soup in the freezer.

Connie's Chicken Soup © Connie Hope

# Connie's Chicken Soup

Left over chicken or fresh chicken with bones and everything
32 oz container of chicken broth (I like the free range type)
Water to cover the chicken bones with Better than Bouillon.
3-4 regular size carrots or 15-20 small carrots, cut in slices
1 1/2 – 2 cups celery
Chicken pieces from the bones
Small pasta or barley, or noodles
½ teaspoon thyme
Chicken bouillon cubes
Salt and pepper to taste
Leftover vegetables if you have them or open your favorite can of green beans, lima beans, or peas.

In a large soup pot, put all the bones with meat.
  (You may have to flatten them a little in the pot)
Add the container of chicken broth and enough water to
  cover the bones.
Put lid on and bring to a boil, then reduce heat so the liquid
  is bubbling slowly.
You can cook it for 2 or 3 hours or more.
Pour the juice and the bones through the strainer/colander.
Transfer the juices to a plastic container and put in the
  refrigerator overnight to allow the fat to congeal.
Let the bones and meat cool in the strainer/colander, then
  pick the meat from the bones and put in the refrigerator.
The next day take out the juice container and skim the fat.
Add the carrots, celery, thyme and any leftover veggie you
  have in the refrigerator.
Cook on medium heat for about 1 hour.
Check after about 30 minutes. Stir. Salt and pepper to taste.
Add the pieces of chicken and the pasta or barley.
Serve with your favorite crispy bread.

# White Bean and Lime Chicken Soup

2 Tablespoons butter
I medium yellow onion, diced
2-3 cloves garlic, minced
I can (7 oz) green chilies, chopped
I Tablespoon  cilantro, chopped
I small Jalapeño pepper, remove veins and seeds *
I can (29 oz) white beans (navy and/or Great Northern)
I can (29 oz) diced tomatoes
I teaspoon oregano
I teaspoon cumin
Dash of cinnamon
Lime juice from I fresh lime (use a reamer) **
I cup chicken pieces-cut in small pieces
8 cups chicken broth
Salt and pepper to taste

Saute butter, onions, and garlic in a large soup pot until translucent,  about 10 minutes.
Add the chopped Jalapeño pepper and green chilies and
    saute for 5 minutes on low heat.
Add chicken broth, tomatoes and beans to onion mixture.
Add cilantro, oregano, cumin, cinnamon diced tomatoes.
Simmer for 30 minutes
Add lime juice and pieces of chicken.
Heat for 5 minutes until chicken is warm.
Serve with garnish of cilantro sprigs.
Serves 4-6

White Bean and Lime Chicken Soup   © Connie Hope  From my novel,
The Bonnie Neuk Tea Room

This is the main soup in my novel, The Bonnie Neuk Tea Room. Victoria Storms serves it in her tea room.

* If you don't want the soup too spicy, eliminate the Jalapeño pepper

I love the taste of this soup.  I like to add additional cilantro. Your choice.

The beans are very flavorful in this soup.  The lime adds a tangy flavor with just a hint of cinnamon and cumin and cilantro.

Here's what I do about chicken and chicken broth.  I get a roasted chicken from the store and have it for dinner.  Then with the leftovers bones and all I put it in a pot with about 8 cups of water and maybe a few chicken bouillon cubes and cook for 3-4 hours slowly.  This will make a great chicken broth.  I use some in this soup and freeze the rest for another pot of soup.

** Check out the Appendix  for information and a
picture about a reamer.
You can also use 2 limes.

*I love this recipe because it has so many great herbs in it.*

Soulful Chicken Soup© Connie Hope

# The Soulful Chicken Soup

Chicken thighs, about 2 pounds, skinned and trimmed
3 carrots, cut ½ inch (about 1 ½ cups)
3 stalks celery, cut in ½ inch pieces (about 2 cups)
1 leek, cleaned and cut thin
2-3 cloves garlic, minced
2 fresh thyme sprigs
2 fresh sage sprigs
1 fresh rosemary sprig
1 bay leaf
Salt and pepper to taste
8 cups of chicken broth
2 cups egg noodles (I like the really wide ones)
3 Tablespoons of fresh parsley, chopped
1 Tablespoon fresh lemon juice

Place chicken and first 9 ingredients in chicken broth.
Cook on simmer for 1 plus hours or until vegetables are tender and
  chicken is done.
Remove chicken from the bones, dice. Return to soup pot.
Stir in noodles and parsley and cook for another 20 minutes
on simmer until noodles are done.  Stir in lemon juice.
Serves 6-8

*The red cherry peppers make this soup spicy. But removing the seeds takes some of the 'heat' out of the peppers.*

# Spiced Chicken Soup

3 Tablespoons olive oil
2 carrots, chopped
2 stalks of celery, chopped
2 cloves of garlic, minced (more if you like garlic)
1 bay leaf
1 onion, finely chopped
2-3 Red cherry peppers, seeded and finely chopped
½ lemon, peel skin off
8 cups chicken broth
2 chicken breast, skinless and boneless
Salt and pepper to taste
4 potatoes, scrubbed well, leave skins on, chop
8 oz cooked pasta (I like the small shells, your choice)

In soup pot, add olive oil and first five ingredients.
Simmer 5-8 minutes. Add cherry peppers, and lemon peel.
Saute for 3-4 minutes add chicken broth and chicken pieces.
Simmer for 30 minutes, add salt and pepper.
Remove chicken and chop. Return to soup pot.
Add potatoes, cover and simmer for 30 minutes, until tender.
Add noodles, cook until tender.  Squeeze lemon and add parsley.
Serves 4

# Southwestern Flair Chicken Soup

1 ( 12 oz) jar salsa verde
3 cups cooked chicken pieces
1 (15 oz) can white beans, drained (cannellini or navy or
    your choice)
3 cups chicken broth (if want thinner, use another cup)
1 teaspoon ground cumin (optional)
3 green onions, chopped
½ cup sour cream
Tortilla chips as a garnish

In a large soup pot, empty the salsa verde.
Heat for 4 minutes over low.
Add the chicken, beans, broth, and cumin.
Bring to a boil, then lower to a simmer.
Cook for 20 minutes low and stir occasionally.
Serve with a garnish of green onion, a spoonful of sour
    cream and tortilla chips for the Southwestern Flair.
Serves 4-5

This recipe is quick and uses up the leftover chicken roaster from the night before.

The cumin really adds a great taste to this soup.

# Ginger Chicken Soup with Vegetables

2 Tablespoons olive oil
1 small red onion, sliced thin
3-4 cloves garlic, minced
3 Tablespoons fresh ginger, grated*
2 (32 oz) boxes of chicken broth
2 parsnips, peeled and chopped
2 carrots, peeled and chopped
2 stalks celery, chopped
2 small turnips, peeled and chopped (about 1 ½ cups)
Salt and pepper to taste
2 ½ to 3 cups rotisserie chicken**
½ cup peas (canned or frozen)
4 scallions, sliced thin
4 biscuits or tasty rolls

Heat oil in soup pot.
Add onions, garlic and ginger and cook 3-4 minutes low.
Stir occasionally.
Add broth, parsnips, carrots, celery, turnips, bring to a boil.
Reduce, simmer until vegetables are tender, 20-25 minutes.
Shred the chicken from the bones, and add the chicken, peas,
    scallions to the soup.
Heat 5-8 minutes so chicken is heated, serve with biscuits.
Serves 4-6

The red onion adds great color to this soup

*You can use jarred ground ginger, but fresh is best.

**Any leftover chicken is good. I usually have the rotisserie chicken for dinner then the next day make a soup.

Instead of the pesto use:

¼ Tablespoon basil, dried
Or
2 Tablespoons fresh
    chopped parsley


You can also add:
2 Tablespoons olive oil
2 med. onions, chopped
1 cup diced carrots
4 teaspoons minced garlic


Saute all added ingredients in oil
and then add the stock and continue with remaining ingredients.

Also can add:
1 can white kidney beans,
    drained
1 cup chopped fresh
    tomatoes

# Tortellini Soup (Basic)

8 cups chicken stock
1 package tortellini either meat or cheese (9 oz pkg)
¾ cup diced, cooked chicken (optional)
2 cups fresh baby spinach, chopped or not chopped (you can
    also use frozen)
4 Tablespoon pesto  *  see appendix for recipe
Salt and pepper to taste
Grated parmesan for topping

Bring chicken stock to a boil.
Add tortellini and chicken pieces, and reduce heat.
Cook for 5-10 minutes.
Add fresh spinach, pesto, salt and pepper to taste.
Serve in a bowl with a sprinkle of parmesan cheese on top.

Tortellini Soup   (copyright by Connie Hope)

# Tortellini with Broccoli

6 chicken breasts, boneless and cooked
1 Tablespoon olive oil
1 cup celery, chopped
1 (8 oz) container of sour cream
1 package (16 oz) frozen broccoli, chopped
1 package (9 oz) fresh cheese tortellini
2 cans ( 10 ¾ oz) cream of chicken soup
3 cans (10 ½ oz) chicken broth
1 large onion, chopped
1 teaspoon basil
Salt and pepper to taste
½ teaspoon Italian seasoning*
¼ teaspoon garlic powder

In a soup pot, add olive oil heated, add onion, celery and
    cook until tender about 15-20 minutes.
Add chicken soup, broth, broccoli, cheese tortellini, salt
    pepper, basil, Italian seasoning and garlic powder.
Bring to a boil, then simmer for 20 minutes.
Stir in sour cream and serve.
Serves  4-5

# Chicken Enchilada Soup

¼ cup olive oil
1 large onion (Vidalia if in season) diced
1 garlic clove, minced
5 cups water (or substitute 3 cups chicken broth for water)
2 teaspoons chicken base (I use Better than Bouillon)
1 teaspoon chili powder
½ teaspoon ground cumin
½ teaspoon cilantro
¼ teaspoon ground coriander
1/8 teaspoon cayenne pepper (or increase, if you like spicier)
1/3 cup masa harina*
8 oz Velveeta cheese cubed
2 cups cooked, cubed chicken breast
¾ cup pico de gallo** (can substitute a can of green chilies)
6 Tablespoons Colby-Monterey Jack cheese, shredded

In a large pot, saute onion in oil until tender.
Add garlic and cook another 2 minutes.
Whisk masa harina and 1 cup of water until smooth.
Stir in pot.
Add the 4 cups of water (or broth) , chicken base, chili
     powder, cumin, coriander and cayenne to the pot.
Bring to a slow boil and stir until thickened.
Reduce heat and stir in Velveeta cubes until melted.
Add chicken and heat thoroughly.
Ladle into bowls and top with shredded cheese and topping.

This is a great soup to use up chicken or turkey leftovers.

*What the heck is Masa Harina?
It is a finely ground corn flour made from corn that has been dried, cooked, ground and dried again. It has it's own distinct flavor.
Masa means dough in Spanish. In this soup it is used as a thickener. You can use regular corn flour, but the taste is not the same.

** Pico de Gallo is a salsa made with chopped tomatoes, white onion, cilantro, lime juice and chilies. You can purchase pre-made at the store or substitute a can of green chilies.

Chicken Enchilada Soup © Connie Hope

- This topping is good, but it takes extra time to put in the plastic bag and then bake.

Variations:

Add a small can of corn
Add a can of black beans
Add a can of Enchilada sauce

The Enchilada sauce adds a little spice to the soup and the corn and black beans add color. I really like this in the soup.

# Easy Topping:

Buy tortilla chips in a bag. They make them in many colors. Crumble them up with cilantro and green onions.

Topping:*
**2 corn tortillas (around 6 inches)**
**½ teaspoon oil**
**½ teaspoon chili powder**
**1/8 teaspoon salt**
**1/8 teaspoon cayenne pepper**

Cut each tortilla lengthwise into thirds.
Then cut each widthwise into ¼ inch strips.
Place strips and oil in a re-sealable plastic bag.
Shake to coat the cut tortilla.
Then add to bag the chili powder, salt, and cayenne pepper.
Shake to coat.
Arrange tortilla strips on a baking sheet coated with cooking spray.
Bake 400 degrees for about 6-8 minutes.
Stir at least once.
Place on a paper towel.

Chicken Enchilada Soup with Black Beans and cheese © Connie Hope

Chicken Enchilada Soup with purple tortilla stripes ©Connie Hope

# Lemony Chicken Soup with Orzo

**Broth:**
1 leftover roasted chicken with 1-2 cups meat
8 cups water
2 bay left
4 teaspoons salt

**Soup:**
1 cup diced onion or leek
1 cup diced celery
1-2 Tablespoons olive oil
2 teaspoons toasted coriander seeds (or ground fine)
¼ cup fresh dill
½ cup lemon juice (2-3 lemons)
Zest from 2 lemons 1 Tablespoon
1 cup orzo
Garnish with sour cream and sprigs of dill (Optional)
2 eggs (if you want to try the variation to the left)

Broth:
Pour 12 cups of water over chicken carcass w/2 bay leaves
Simmer covered for 1-2 hours.
Strain over a large bowl, reserving stock and meat.
Let cool. Then separate meat from bones.
Soup:
In pot, saute onion and celery in oil until tender, 5 minutes.
Add chicken stock and meat.
Add coriander seed, dill, and lemon zest.
Bring to a boil. Reduce.
Add orzo and let simmer uncovered 15-20 minutes.
Add the lemon juice. Heat for 5 minutes.
Serve in bowls with sour cream, sprig of dill.
Serves 8

There are several kinds of Orzo. I like the Tri-color, but all taste good.

Variation:

Add ¼ teaspoon marjoram

Variation: **Lemony Chicken and Egg Soup**

One recipe I found used 2 eggs in the soup.
Take out 2 cups broth.
In a medium bowl whisk 2 large eggs and ½ cup fresh lemon juice. Whisk well.
Very gradually, while whisking the egg mixture vigorously, slowly drizzle the two cups of hot broth into the egg mixture.
You don't want the eggs to curdle. BE VERY CAREFUL, VERY SLOW. Then pour into the pot and slowly mix well.
Heat for 5 minutes and serve.

Lemony Chicken Soup with Orzo ©Connie Hope

Dumplings:
3 egg whites
½ cup cottage cheese
2 Tablespoons water
Salt and pepper to taste
1 cup flour

You can substitute a Vidalia onion, chopped, for the shallots.

Chunky style

# Chicken Dumpling Soup

1 pound  boneless chicken breasts, skinned and cubed
2 boxes (32 oz) chicken broth
3 cups water
4-5 carrots, chopped
2 stalks of celery, chopped
1 teaspoon fresh parsley
Salt and pepper to taste
¼ teaspoon garlic powder*
¼ teaspoon poultry seasoning

Coat soup pot with cooking spray and cook chicken.
Add the broth, water, vegetables and seasonings.
Bring to boil, then simmer for 40 minutes until tender.
Dumplings: beat egg whites & cottage cheese until blended.
Set aside. Add water, salt and pepper to pot.
Stir in flour and mix well. Bring liquid soup back to a boil.
Drop dumplings by the Tablespoonful into the boiling soup.
Reduce heat, cover, simmer for 15 minutes or until a tooth
   pick inserted in a dumpling comes out clean.
Serves 4

# Cream of Chicken Soup

3 Tablespoons of butter
4 Shallots, chopped*
1 leek, sliced thin
1 pound chicken breast, boneless and cooked
2 ½ cups chicken broth
1 teaspoon fresh parsley, chopped
1 teaspoon fresh thyme
Salt and pepper to taste
3/4 cup heavy cream
Sprigs of thyme for garnish

Melt butter in a soup pot. Add shallots, cook for 3-4 minutes.
Add the chicken, broth, the herbs, salt, and pepper.
Bring to boil, simmer for 30 minutes. Cool 15 minutes.
Using a blender or an immersing blender, puree the mixture.
Return to the pot, add the cream and heat for 5 minutes.
Stir occasionally.  Add thyme for garnishing.
Serve 4-5

# Chicken Noodle Soup

2 chicken breasts, boneless and skinless.
5 cups of chicken broth
3 carrots, peeled and cut in ¼ inch pieces
2 Stalks celery, cut in ¼ inch pieces
Salt and pepper to taste
½ teaspoon tarragon or thyme
1 cup noodles or vermicelli (break in half or quarters)

In a soup pot, put chicken breast, broth, cook for 30 minutes.
Remove the chicken from the broth.
Add carrots, celery, salt, pepper, cook until tender.
Cut chicken breast into cubes, return to pot, add the noodles.
Simmer until noodles are done, 5-7 minutes.
Serve with tarragon or thyme as garnish.
Serves 4-5

# Chicken and Rice Soup

6 ¼ cups chicken broth
2 carrots, peeled and thinly sliced
2 stalks of celery
1 leek, cut very thin
1 (4 oz) can small peas (or frozen, but use small peas)
1 cup cooked rice
6 oz cooked chicken, cubed or chunked
2 teaspoons fresh tarragon*
1 Tablespoon fresh parsley
Salt and pepper to taste

Put broth in a soup pot, add the carrots, celery, leeks.
Bring to a boil, reduce, simmer covered for 10 minutes.
Add the peas, rice and chicken and simmer for 10 minutes or
    until veggies are tender.
Add the tarragon, parsley, salt and pepper. Simmer for 10
    minutes. Garnish with parsley.
Serves 4-5

Leeks can retain dirt. Always wash or rinse thoroughly under water.

*If you are using dried tarragon it is a little less than 1 teaspoon

Use any type of rice you like.

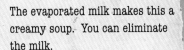

The evaporated milk makes this a creamy soup. You can eliminate the milk.

I used wild rice in this soup which adds an interesting flavor.

# Chicken and Potato Soup

4 cups diced potatoes
1 medium onion, chopped
3-4 Tablespoons olive oil
1 ½ cups chopped cooked chicken
2 cups chicken broth
2 teaspoons fresh parsley
Salt and pepper to taste
1 large can evaporated milk (about 1 2/3 cup)

Saute potatoes and onion in oil.
Add chicken, chicken broth, parsley, salt and pepper.
Heat to a boil and lower heat.
Cover, simmer until potatoes are tender, about 30 minutes.
Stir in evaporated milk.
Serves 4-5

# Hearty Chicken Vegetable Soup

2-3 pounds of chicken breast, cut in cubes
1 Tablespoon oil
1 large onion, chopped
5 stalks celery, chopped, 1 inch long
5 carrots, chopped 1 inch long
3-4 cloves of garlic, minced
6 cups chicken broth
Salt and pepper to taste
2 bay leaves
3 sprigs fresh thyme or 3 Tablespoons dried thyme)
1 cup peas (canned or frozen)
Egg noodles (or rice)

In a soup pot, combine oil, onion, celery, carrot, garlic.
Simmer for 5-8 minutes until tender.
Add chicken and spices and simmer 5 minutes.
Cover with broth, bring to a boil, simmer for 30 minutes.
In a separate pot, cook the noodles (or rice) until al dente.
Add to soup pot and cook for 5 minutes.
Serves 5-6

# Fifteen (15) Bean Soup*

1 pound chicken, cubed
1 pound sausage, sliced ¼ inch, cooked, and drained
½ cup onion, diced
½ cup celery, diced
½ cup carrots, diced
1-2 garlic cloves
8 cups chicken broth
2 Tablespoons butter

Cover beans with water and soak overnight.
Drain beans.
In a soup pot, add chicken broth and bring beans to a boil.
Reduce heat and simmer uncovered for 2 hours.
In a frying pan, melt butter and saute onion, celery, carrot,
    garlic and chicken over medium heat for 10-15 minutes
    or until vegetables are tender.
Add chicken, sliced sausage and any spices to the broth and
    beans and simmer for 30-40 minutes.
Salt and pepper to taste.
Serves 10

Fifteen Bean Soup © Connie Hope

Fifteen (15) Bean soup can be purchased as a one bag soup. There are
many possibilities for ingredients,
but the bag has a great recipe on it.

If I have other vegetables in my
refrigerator, I add them also–sometimes zucchini or broccoli or even
potatoes.

You can add herbs of your choice:
Oregano
Basil
Marjoram
Thyme

*These beans are in the bag of 15
bean soup:
Northern
Pinto
Large Lima
Black eye peas
Garbanzo
Baby Lima
Green split peas
Kidney
Cranberry
Small white
Pink Beans
Small red
Yellow split pea
Lentil
Navy
White kidney
Black beans

The amounts shown are to be used as a guideline.
Use what ever ingredients you have on hand and how much you want. Soup is forgiving.

My mother just made the soup after the 4 hours. I put the broth in the refrigerator overnight. This way the fat will form on the top and I can remove it.

# Mom's Turkey Soup

The soup is prepared in two steps. The first step is making the turkey stock and then the turkey soup.

For the stock:
Remove all usable turkey meat from the carcass.
If your carcass is very large, you might want to break up
    the bones a bit.
Place carcass in a large soup pot.
Cover the carcass with about 4-6 quarts of water or
    chicken or turkey broth (if you are lucky enjoy to find it)
**Add:   1 medium onion cut in wedges.**
       **1 to 2 carrots, roughly chopped**
       **A few sprigs of parsley**
       **1-2 sprigs of thyme or a teaspoon of dried thyme**
       **1 bay leaf**
       **1 large celery, cut in several pieces including**
          **the tops**

Bring to a boil and lower the heat to a simmer.
It may foam, so remove the foam immediately.
Cook for at least 4 hours—covered at first, then
    uncovered.
Remove foam as it appears.
After at least 4 hours, strain broth and refrigerate.
Refrigerate bones to cool, then remove all meat for soup.

**Making the Turkey Soup:**
**In a large soup pot, heat a little butter or olive oil.**
**Add:**
  **1 to 1 ½ cups each, chopped carrots, onion, and celery**
  **Fresh sprigs of parsley, chopped**
  **A few cloves of garlic, minced**
  **2 cups of turkey, chopped**
  **Salt and pepper to taste**
  **1 Teaspoon, sage, thyme, or marjoram.**
  **Pasta, barley or rice when soup is almost complete**

Remove the broth from refrigerator and skim off fat.
Pour the liquid over the veggies in the large soup pot.
Simmer for at least an hour or until veggies are tender.
Add your rice, barley or pasta—as little or as much as
    you'd like.
Serve hot.
Serves 4-6

# Turkey Meatball Soup

10-15 frozen meat balls or make fresh turkey meatballs
2 ½ cups chicken broth(or turkey broth if you can find it)
1 can (14 oz) stewed tomatoes
2   medium zucchini, cleaned, chopped in pieces
2   carrots, thinly sliced
2/3 cup corn (frozen or canned)
½ cup green bean (frozen or canned)
1 teaspoon dried basil
Salt and pepper to taste.

In a large soup pot, combine water or chicken broth, stewed
    tomatoes, zucchini, carrots, corn, green beans, basil, salt
    and pepper.
Bring to a boil, then simmer, cover for 20 minutes.
Vegetables should be tender.   Add meatballs, simmer until tender about
20 minutes.
Serve 5-6

# Chunky Turkey and Vegetable Soup

1 Tablespoon olive oil
1 onion, finely chopped
2-3 cloves of garlic, minced
2-3 Tablespoons tomato paste (I use a tube of tomato paste,
    it stores better)
1 large sweet potato, peeled and chunked
1 (14.5 oz) can diced tomato with juice
2 (14.5 oz) can chicken broth (use turkey if you can find it)
½ teaspoon dried rosemary
1 pound cooked turkey breast, cut into chunks
1 head escarole, washed, trimmed,  torn into small pieces
Salt and pepper to taste

In a soup pot, heat oil and add onion and garlic.
Cook, stirring occasionally, about 5-6 minutes.
Stir in tomato paste.
Add sweet potato, tomatoes, juice, broth, and rosemary.
Bring to boil, reduce, simmer for 15 minutes, until veggie
    are tender.
Stir in turkey, salt, pepper, and add escarole in two batches,
Cover, simmer for 5-6 minutes.
Serves 5-6

In any soup you can always use water instead of broth.  I just feel that broth adds much more flavor.

If you wanted to put this in a crock pot, you can cook on Low for 8 hours.

Variations:

1 small fennel bulb, chopped fine
1 (14.5 oz) can diced tomatoes

The kinds of beans are the same for any 15 bean bag for soups

# Turkey Kielbasa Soup

½ pound turkey kielbasa, sliced
1 Tablespoon olive oil
1 medium onion, chopped
1 medium green pepper, chopped
2 stalks celery, chopped
4-5 cloves of garlic, minced
2 cans (14 ½ oz) chicken broth
1 can great northern beans, rinsed and drained
1 can (14 ½ oz) stewed tomatoes, chopped
1 small zucchini, peeled and sliced
1 medium carrot, shredded
1 Tablespoon dried parsley
¼ teaspoon red pepper flakes
Salt and pepper to taste

Put olive oil in a skillet, cook kielbasa over medium heat
    until lightly browned.
Add onions, green pepper, and celery.
Simmer, stir and cook for 5 minutes.
Add garlic and cook for 4 minutes.
Put all ingredients in a large soup pot.
Cover and cook for 1 hour, stirring occasionally.
Make sure that vegetables are tender.
Serves 4-5

# Turkey 15 Bean Soup

1 large onion, diced (sweet onion or Vidalia onion is best)
½ stick butter
4 carrots, sliced ¼ inch
2-3 stalks celery, diced
2-3 cloves of garlic  (can use garlic powder)
Bay leaf
2 teaspoons sage
8 cups chicken broth (use turkey broth if you can find it or
    Better than Bouillon)
1 (20 oz bag) of 15 Beans bag (rinsed and soaked in
    water for at least 1 hour) rinse and drain
2 turkey wings or legs, boil for 10 minutes and remove skin
    (or use the leftover turkey)1 ½-2 cups turkey meat

Saute onion, carrots, celery, and garlic in butter, 5-6
    minutes.
Add broth, beans, spices and cook low for 1-2 hours or until
    beans are tender.
Remove the bay leaf.
Add cooked turkey, and simmer for 10 minutes.
Serves 5-6

# Beef Barley Soup

1 ½ to 2 pounds ground beef
2 medium onions, chopped
½ cup celery, chopped
3 cups water ( or beef broth)
1 box beef broth, (32 oz)
1 cup barley
2 cans (14 ½ oz) diced tomatoes with basil and garlic
2 teaspoons Worcestershire sauce
Salt and pepper to taste
1 teaspoon dried basil

In soup pot, cook the ground beef, onions, and celery over
   medium heat until no longer pink, drain.
Stir in water and broth, bring to a boil, then reduce.
Add barley, cover and simmer for 30 minutes until tender.
Stir in tomatoes, Worcestershire sauce, salt, pepper and basil.
Stir and simmer for 20-30 minutes.
Serves 4-6

# Hearty Beef Barley Soup

2 Tablespoons flour
Salt and pepper
1 pound top sirloin steak, cubed
1 Tablespoon olive oil
2 cups fresh mushrooms, cut in pieces
1 box (32 oz) beef broth
3 medium carrots, sliced in ½ inch pieces
1-2 cloves of garlic, minced
¼ teaspoon dried thyme
½ cup barley

In a plastic bag combine, flour, salt and pepper.
Add beef and shake to coat.
In a soup pot, brown beef in oil until meat is tender.
Remove beef and set aside.
In same pot, saute mushrooms and garlic until tender.
Add the broth, carrots, thyme and bring to a boil.
Reduce heat to a simmer and add barley and beef.
Cover and simmer for 30 minutes.
Serves 4-6

You can put this in containers
and freeze for a later time.

This uses sirloin steak cubes
instead of ground beef.

This soup is a complete meal in a bowl. I'd even call it a stew, but it has been labeled a soup in my recipe files.

There is nothing like this on a cold day. Hearty and very tasty.

*I use the tube of Italian seasoning.

# Beef and Sausage Soup

1 pound beef stew meat, cubed
1 Tablespoon olive oil
1 pound loose, sweet sausage
1 can (28 oz) diced tomatoes
3 ½ cups water ( or use beef broth)
1 cup onions, chopped
1 Tablespoon Worcestershire Sauce
Salt and pepper to taste
1/2 teaspoon Italian seasoning*
2 cups, cubed, peeled potatoes
1 cup celery, chopped

In a large soup pot, brown beef cubes in oil.
Remove with a slotted spoon and set aside.
Brown sausage and onions on all sides, drain.
Return beef cubes, onions and sausage to the pot
Add tomatoes, water (or broth), and seasoning.
Bring to a boil then reduce, cover and simmer for 1 ½ hours.
Add potatoes and celery, cover and cook 30 minutes.
Potatoes and celery should be tender.
Serves 6-7

Beef and Sausage Soup © Connie Hope

# Beef Barley Soup with Roasted Vegetables

¼ cup flour
Salt and pepper to taste
I pound beef stew meat, cut in I inch cubes
5 Tablespoons olive oil, separated
I Portobello mushroom, large, remove stem and chop
I medium onion, chopped
I fennel bulb, chopped
1-2 cloves garlic, minced
8 cups beef stock
2 cups water
2 cups butternut squash, peeled and cubed
I large potato, peeled and cubed
2 large carrots, peeled and cut in ½ inch pieces
2/3 cup barley
2 teaspoons fresh thyme
½ teaspoon marjoram
¼ teaspoon nutmeg
¼ cup fresh parsley, minced, just the tops

In a plastic baggie, mix flour, salt, and pepper.
Put beef in baggie and toss to coat.
In a soup pot, heat 2 Tablespoons oil over medium heat.
Add the beef and brown on all sides. Remove
In the same pan, heat I Tablespoon oil and add mushrooms,
    onions and fennel.
Cook and stir over medium heat until tender for 5 minutes.
Stir in garlic for about I minute.
Add stock & water, loosen browned bits at bottom.
Return beef and bring to a boil, reduce heat.
Cover and simmer for I hour or until meat is tender.
At the same time, place the squash, potato and carrots on a
    greased baking pan.
Drizzle with remaining oil, toss to coat veggies.
Bake at 425 for 20-25 minutes until veggies are tender.
Add barley, thyme, marjoram, nutmeg, and roasted
    vegetables to soup.
Return to boil, cover and simmer for15 minutes or until
    barley is tender.  Sprinkle with parsley.
Serves 6-8

Cooking two things at once is timesaving.

While you are simmering the soup, you can roast the veggies in the oven.

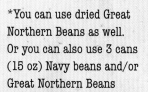

*You can use dried Great Northern Beans as well. Or you can also use 3 cans (15 oz) Navy beans and/or Great Northern Beans

I like this sometimes without the tomatoes.

This is a thick soup. If you want to thin it, add additional beef broth or chicken broth.

# Bean and Bacon Soup

1 (16 oz) package dried navy beans*
2 onions, chopped
2 stalks celery, chopped
2 Cloves of garlic, minced
1 large potato cubed
½ pound sliced bacon
Salt and pepper to taste
3 carrots, peeled and sliced
4 cups of vegetable broth
1 bay leaf
1 sprig of fresh thyme (or use 1 teaspoon dried thyme)
2 (8 oz) cans diced tomatoes

Boil the beans in 9 cups of water and let stand for 1 hour.
Drain and set aside (or use canned beans).
Cook bacon in a soup pot and set on a paper towel to drain.
When it cools, chop it up.
Discard all but about ¼ cup of the bacon fat.
Add onions, celery, garlic, potato to fat, cook for 5 minutes.
Add broth, diced tomatoes, bay leaf and thyme and simmer
    for 20-30 minutes.
Remove the bay leaf and sprig of thyme.
Serves 5-6

# Beef Barley and Mushroom Soup

1 ½ pounds of beef cubes
1 Tablespoon olive oil
2 cups yellow onions, chopped finely
1 cup carrots, diced
½ cup celery, diced
1 pound fresh mushrooms, sliced
2-3 cloves garlic, minced
½ teaspoon dried thyme  (use more if fresh)
1 (14 ½ oz) can beef broth
1 (14 ½ oz) can chicken broth
2 cups water
½ cup medium barley
Salt and pepper to taste
¼ cup fresh parsley, chopped

In soup pot put oil; brown beef cubes on all sides.
Remove and set aside.
Saute onion, carrots, celery in drippings until tender.
Add mushrooms, garlic and thyme. Stir, cook 3-5 minutes.
Stir in broth, water, barley, salt and pepper. Add beef cubes.  Bring to boil.
Simmer 2 plus hours.  Add parsley.
Serves 4-5

# Mushroom Beef Soup

1 medium yellow onion, chopped
2/3 – 1 cup mushrooms, sliced
2 Tablespoons flour
2-3 cups beef broth (homemade or canned)
2/3 – 1 cup cubed cooked roast beef *
½ teaspoon garlic powder
¼ teaspoon paprika
Salt and pepper to taste
¼ cup finely, chopped parsley
Dash of pepper sauce or hot sauce
¼ cup shredded mozzarella cheese (optional)

In a soup pot sauté  beef cubes. Set aside
Sauté onions and mushrooms in same pot until tender.
Remove and set aside.
Whisk flour and broth gradually in the soup pot until
    smooth.
Bring to a slow boil, then stir for 1-2 minutes.
Broth should start to thicken.
Add beef, garlic powder, paprika salt, pepper, pepper sauce,
    and onion-mushroom mix.
Heat while stirring continually.
Serve hot.
Top with mozzarella cheese (optional).

# Meatball Soup

¼ cup finely chopped onion
2 Tablespoons olive oil
4-5 cups beef broth (homemade or canned)
1 can (16 oz) kidney beans rinsed and drained (can use
    green beans or pinto beans)
1 can (14 oz) stewed tomatoes
10-15 frozen or freshly made meatballs (see recipe at right)
1 medium carrot, sliced thin or 10-15 baby carrots
1 teaspoon Italian seasoning
¼ cup uncooked small shell pasta

In a soup pot simmer olive oil and onion.
Cook onion until translucent.
Then add remaining ingredients except pasta.
Add meatballs and simmer slowly.
Bring to a boil, then reduce heat, cover, simmer for 15
    minutes.
Add pasta, simmer 15 minutes or until pasta is tender.
Serves 5-6.
Sprinkle with parmesan cheese

*This is a great use of left-
    over pot roast or steak.

Or just use fresh cubed
stewing meat.  Use 2 Tablespoons olive oil in a large soup,
sauté meat on all sides.

This could almost be called a
stew.  If you want it thinner, add
more beef broth.

How to Make Fresh Meatballs

1 egg slightly beaten
¼ cup corn flake crumbs
¼ cup finely chopped
    parsley
Salt and pepper to taste
½ pound lean ground beef
2 Tablespoons olive oil

Mix all ingredients.
Shape into 1 inch balls.
Brown in saucepan with oil or
microwave for 1 minute, then
turn and do another minute.
Drain on paper towel.

* You can use beef stock or a combination if you would like.

# Kitchen Sink Soup

1 pound lean chopped meat, cooked and fat drained
1 cup each of any 4-5 of your favorite vegetables and any
    juice (such as carrots, green beans, peas, wax beans,
    zucchini, lima beans )
1 cup pasta, cooked ( leftover pasta is great)
4 cups beef stock
Salt and pepper to taste
Dash of Tabasco sauce or green pepper sauce

Combine everything except the pasta in a soup pot.
Cook at medium heat until it starts to bubble.
Turn low and simmer for 1 ½ hours.
Add pasta and cook another 15 minutes or until tender.
Serve with crusty bread.
Serves 4-6

# Couscous Meatball Soup

1 pound ground beef
2 teaspoons dried basil
2 teaspoons dried oregano
Salt and pepper to taste
1 large onion, finely chopped
2 Tablespoons olive oil
8 cups collard greens, chopped
8 cups of kale, chopped
2 boxes (32 oz each) vegetable broth*
1 Tablespoon white wine vinegar
½ teaspoon red pepper flakes
1 package (about 8.8 oz) couscous

In a bowl combine the beef, basil, oregano, salt and pepper.
Shape into meat balls.
Spray cooking oil in a skillet and brown meatballs.
Or put them in microwave on a plate, cook until browned.
In the skillet, brown onion in the oil.
Add collards and kale, cook 8 minutes or until wilted.
In a soup pot combine the greens mixture, meatballs, stock,
    vinegar, couscous, pepper flakes, salt and pepper to taste.
Bring to a boil, then reduce to a simmer for 15-20 minutes
    or until the couscous is tender.
Stir occasionally.
Serves 8.

# Connie's Cooking Tips

• If you need a thickener for soups or stews, use just a little of the instant mash potatoes (the one in the box).

• If you have trouble digesting beans (the old tooting problem), add several stalks of celery, chopped and it should help.

• When have finished cooking vegetables or potatoes, save the liquid in a plastic container. Put it in the freezer and continue to add to it until you have enough to add to you next homemade soup. It adds great favor to whatever soup you are cooking.

• In fact, if I have a few vegetables that are not used after the meal, I add it to that broth for the next time I make soup. I get a great feeling from not wasting food.

• To keep the grains of rice from sticking together, a drop or two of lemon juice should help.

• Fresh lemon juice can remove most of the onion and even garlic smell from your hands. Now don't go overboard, just a few drops will help.

• If you are in need of a quick ice pack for a minor accident around the house, grab a bag of frozen beans or peas or any vegetable from the freezer and put it on the bump.

Garlic © Connie Hope

Group of Onions © Connie Hope

Instead of water you can use vegetable broth

*You can add more clams if you like the soup thick with them.

# Clam Chowder

4 ounces salt pork, diced
1 small onion, finely diced
¼ cup celery, diced
3 medium potatoes, peeled and chopped small
1 cup clam juice
1 cup water
Salt and Pepper to taste
¼ teaspoon dried thyme (I use a little more as I love thyme)
2 cups milk
2 cups light cream
4 dozen clams (or as much as you like)

In a large soup pot, brown salt pork and remove.
In the soup pot saute onion and celery until tender.
Add potatoes, clam juice, water, thyme, salt and pepper.
Simmer uncovered until potatoes are tender, 20-30 minutes.
Stir in milk, cream, slowly and add clams.
Heat another 15 minutes, but do not boil.
Serves 4

# Clam and Sausage Chowder

2 pounds smoked sausage, thinly sliced
1 medium onion, diced
2-3 garlic cloves, minced
2 Tablespoons olive oil
1 ½ pounds of potatoes, cubed
10 ounces whole kernel corn frozen or canned
4 bottles clam juice (8 oz each)
2 cups water
1 teaspoon fennel seeds-crushed
½ teaspoon red pepper
2 (16 oz) cans tomatoes , crushed or diced
2 dozen fresh, shells cleaned, clams or 2-3 cans of clams*
½ cup fresh parsley, cut just the tops

Wash clams thoroughly, discard any opened shells. Set aside.
Brown sausage in large soup pot, then drain on paper towel.
Cook onions and garlic in olive oil over medium heat.
Add potatoes, corn,clam juice, water, fennel, and red pepper.
Bring to a boil, then reduce heat and simmer for 15-20
    minutes or until potatoes are tender. Stir in tomatoes.
Remove about 2 cups of mixture and put in blender or
    immerse blender, process until smooth.
Return to pot and bring to a boil.  Add clams, reduce heat
    and simmer 5-6 minutes Discard unopened shells. Stir in
    sausage and parsley, heat 5 minutes.
Serves 5-6.

# New England Clam Chowder

10 slices bacon , chopped
1 medium onion, diced
½ cup celery, diced
3 potatoes, peeled and diced
2 cups clam juice
Salt and pepper to taste
1 Tablespoon dried thyme
1 bay leaf
2 cups milk
2 cups light cream
2 Tablespoon cornstarch
2 dozen fresh clams or 2 cans (5 oz or 6 ½ oz whole clams)
Reserve juice from cans of clams

In a soup pot, brown bacon then remove.
Saute onion and celery until tender.
Add potatoes, clam juice, thyme, bay leaf, salt, and pepper.
Make a paste with 2 Tablespoons cornstarch and clam juice.
Set aside. Stir in milk, cream and clams. Remove bay leaf.
Heat until hot, but Do Not Boil. If you like chowder thicker,
    add the paste of cornstarch, stir slowly.
Serves 4-5

# Connie's Clam Chowder

8 slices bacon-chopped
½ cup celery, chopped
½ cup onion, chopped
2 cups diced raw potatoes
Salt and pepper
1 can tomatoes, chopped
¼- ½ teaspoon thyme
2 teaspoons minced parsley
2 cans minced clams ( 18 steamers)
2-3 cups water  (I use clam broth)

Brown bacon in large kettle.
Add celery and onions, sauté slowly.
Add thyme, parsley, tomatoes, water or clam broth.
Cook 10 minutes. Add potatoes, cook until done.
Add clams, salt and pepper to taste.
Serves  4-6

This is similar to Connie's Clam Chowder that is in my first cookbook, In Addition...to the Entrée.  That one does not contain the milk or cream.

* You can add 1 clove of garlic.
Substitution:
Eliminate one cup milk and use 1 can cream of celery soup.

1 teaspoon dill can be added
1 teaspoon hot pepper sauce to add a little heat.

I entered this recipe in our Mother of Twins Cookbook that was published in 1985.

Variation:
1 cup carrots, diced

Thanks, Ginny.  This is really great!!

Recipe can be doubled if you are having lots of people over.

*Can use about 3 cups, peeled, seeded and chopped fresh tomatoes.

Optional:
Can also add 1 pound of cooked shrimp, chopped into 1/3's.
This makes the soup very rich.

# Manhattan Clam Chowder

2 dozen clams or 2  (6 ½ oz) cans minced clams
6 slices bacon, chopped
2 cups onions, finely chopped
1 cup celery, chopped
1 cup green pepper, chopped
1 cup carrots, chopped
1   (28 or 29 oz)can crushed tomatoes*
1 Tablespoon garlic clove, chopped
1 bay leaf
1 teaspoon thyme
Salt and pepper to taste
½ cup fresh parsley, chopped
4 potatoes, peeled and cubed
½ teaspoon crushed red pepper
1 teaspoon dried oregano
3 cups clam broth or water

Steam clams or open can of clams.
Chop clams, and reserve liquid and add water or clam juice
    to make 3 cups.
In a soup pot, add bacon and cook over medium heat until
    slightly crispy.
Add onions, garlic and cook until transparent.
Add peppers, carrots, and celery.
Simmer for 3-5 minutes or until tender.
Add clams, tomatoes, clam liquid, bay leaf, thyme, salt and
    pepper.  Bring to a boil.
Add potatoes, simmer for 30 minutes or until potatoes
    are tender.   Remove bay leaf.
Add chopped parsley.
Add the shrimp if you are using them. Simmer for a few more minutes.
Serves 4-6

# Scallop Chowder

1 (12 oz) package fresh or frozen scallops
3 cups boiling water
Salt and pepper to taste
2 cups potatoes, peeled and cubed
1 cup carrots, peeled and chopped
1 cup celery, chopped
1 medium yellow onion, chopped
1 cup milk
1 cup chicken broth
1 Tablespoon butter
Parsley or lemon slices for garnishing

Cook scallops in boiling water for 3-4 minutes.
Cut in smaller pieces if they are large scallops.
Remove from water, reserve liquid, Set scallops aside.
Add potatoes, carrots, celery and onion to water.
Simmer until tender (10-12 minutes).
Stir in milk, chicken broth, salt and pepper and butter.
Puree in blender using only ½ cup of the scallops.
Return to pot, add remaining scallops and reheat.
Garnish with parsley or try lemon slices.
Serves 6

# Creamy Seafood Bisque

½ cup butter, cubed
1 red onion, chopped
1 cup fresh mushrooms, sliced
2-3 cloves of garlic, minced
½ cup flour
Salt and pepper to taste
2 Tablespoons tomato paste*
1 box (32 oz) chicken broth
2 cups baby clams, whole, and drained
½ pound uncooked, medium shrimp, peeled and deveined
2 cups lump crabmeat, drained
2 cup heavy whipping cream
½ cup Parmesan cheese, shredded
2 green onions, sliced thin for garnish

In a soup pot, heat butter and add red onion and mushrooms.
Saute for 5-7 minutes or until tender.
Add garlic and cook 1-2 minutes longer.
Stir in flour, salt and pepper until blended. Add tomato paste.
Gradually whisk into broth and bring to a boil.
Reduce and simmer for 8-10 minutes.
Add clams and shrimp and bring back to a boil.
Reduce and simmer for 10 minutes or until shrimp are pink.
Stir in crab and cream, heat until warm.
Garnish with cheese and green onions.
Serves 6-8

Chowder is a hearty soup made from a variety of ingredientsL most often it is seafood and milk. The word "chowder" is taken from the French word "Chaudière", a large heavy kettle used to make soups and stews.

* I get the tomato paste in a tube. It stays for several weeks in the refrigerator.

Variations:

1 teaspoon oregano
¼ teaspoon cayenne
   pepper
½ cup uncooked small pasta,
   add with shrimp

Tomato Paste © Connie Hope

Variation:
1 cup light coconut milk instead of
1 cup chicken broth.

Or another option is

¼ teaspoon red curry paste

Once again this recipe is from my
mother, Blanche.
She loved to make soup.

Thanks, Mom

# Shrimp Soup

2 Tablespoons olive oil
1 Tablespoon green onion,  chopped
1 green pepper, diced
1 cup celery, diced
1 clove garlic, minced
1 teaspoon Worcestershire sauce
Dash of Tabasco
2 cups chicken broth
1 (46 oz ) tomato juice
2 Tablespoons rosemary
½ teaspoon fennel seeds.
2 bay leaves
1 cup white wine  (optional)
1 pound large shrimp, deveined and cleaned

In a soup pot, saute in oil, green onion, green pepper, celery,
    garlic until translucent.
Pour broth Worcestershire sauce, Tabasco, chicken broth,
    tomato juice and spices into pot.
Bring to a boil and reduce heat and simmer one hour.
Stir in wine and simmer another hour.
Stir in shrimp and continue cooking for 3-5 minutes or until
    shrimp are done.
Serve with crusty bread.
Serves 6-8

Shrimp Soup© Connie Hope

# Lobster Bisque (or Crab Bisque)

1 medium onion, chopped
½ cup butter
¾ cup flour
4 cups chicken broth (one box 32 ox)
¾ cup dry sherry (you can substitute white wine)
2 lobster tails, cubed ( about 2 cups lobster) *
3 cups light cream
2 Tablespoons tomato paste
Salt and pepper to taste
Parsley for garnishing (optional)

Saute onion in butter.
Stir in flour and cook until bubbles start.
Slowly add broth and wire whisk until thick.
Stir in sherry and lobster.
Cover and simmer for 15-20 minutes.
Stir in cream, tomato paste and salt and pepper.
Simmer another 10 minutes so the cream is warm.
Add parsley for garnishing.
Serves 6-8

# Scallop Bisque

1 pound sea scallops, small or large
1 Tablespoon onions, finely chopped
3 Tablespoons butter
2 Tablespoons flour
3 cups milk
Salt ant pepper to taste
1 garlic clove, finely minced
1 bay leaf

Rinse and chop scallops into halves or thirds (if you have
    used the larger scallops).
Melt butter and saute onions, until translucent.
Whisk flour into the butter and onion mix.
Gradually stir and add the milk.
Simmer until thickened.
Add salt, pepper, garlic, bay leaf and scallops.
Cook over low heat for 20-30 minutes.
Remove bay leaf and serve
Serves 4

*This can also be a Crab Bisque.
Substitute 2 cans crab meat, drained for
the lobster

Also you can use a whole lobster and
clean out all the meat.

Can use an immersion blender and make
it smooth.

Additions:
If you like a little heat, put in a pinch of
ground cayenne pepper.

This recipe also is interchangable with
the Lobster Bisque above. This one does
not have the sherry and serves only 4.

# Fish Chowder

2 ½ pound fish (white fish of your choice)
¼ pound salt pork
1 large onion, diced
½ cup celery
3 medium potatoes, cubed
1 teaspoon Old Bay
1 Tablespoon fresh thyme ( or 1 teaspoon dried thyme)
1 quart milk, or half and half
Salt and pepper
Butter

Cover fish with water.
Boil for 10 minutes.
Remove fish, skin and bones.
Put salt pork in large pot, add onion, potatoes, and brown.
Add spices. Simmer until soft.
Add fish and milk.
Heat and season.

## Fish Chowder Variation

4 ½ cups water (or use 2 cups clam juice)
4 bay leaves
1 ½ pounds halibut fillet or other firm white fish, skinned
3 slices bacon, uncooked
3 cups baking potato, peeled and cubed
1 ½ cups onion, chopped
½ cup carrot, chopped
1 ½ teaspoons dried thyme
Salt and pepper to taste
4 cups milk (reduced fat or regular)
1 Tablespoon butter, cut into pieces

Bring the water and bay leaves to a simmer in a soup pot.
Add fish, cover and simmer 15 minutes or until fish flakes.
Remove fish with a slotted spoon.
Cut fish into large chunks. Reserve 2 ½ cups liquid and bay
   leaves.
Cook bacon in the same pot until crisp.
Remove bacon, reserving 1 teaspoon drippings in pan.
Add potato, onion, & carrot cook medium heat 10 minutes.
Add reserve water, bay leaves and thyme. Salt and pepper to
   taste. Bring to a boil.
Reduce and simmer for 10 minutes.  Add milk and butter and
   simmer for 30 minutes or until potatoes are tender.
Stir in fish. Salt and pepper to taste.  Discard bay leaves.
Sprinkle with bacon.

Thanks, Mom

Serve with oyster crackers.

You can add 1 teaspoon Old Bay
seasoning.

I like to add fresh parsley ends.

# Clam and Leek Bisque

2 cups leeks, minced
¼ cup celery
¼ cup onion
2-3 cloves of garlic, minced
3 Tablespoons carrots, minced
4 Tablespoons butter
4 cups beef stock
I to I ½ cup diced potatoes
I 7 ½ oz can clams, minced and liquid
I 7 ½ oz can chopped clams and liquid
I cup half and half cream.
Salt and pepper to taste
Parsley minced finely

Saute leeks, celery, onion, garlic, carrots in butter until soft.
Add stock and potatoes.
Cover, bring to a boil, then simmer until potatoes are tender.
Puree in blender or use a immerse blender.
Combine potato mixture with clams and add cream.
Reheat, but do not boil.  Season to taste.
Sprinkle with lots of finely minced parsley.
Garnish with crackers.
Serves 4-5

# Clam and Corn Chowder

I (10 oz) can clams, chopped, drain, and rinsed
2-3 Tablespoons dry white wine
4 teaspoon butter
I large onion, finely chopped
I carrot, finely chopped
3 Tablespoons flour
2 cup clam juice
I pounds potatoes, peeled and diced
I cup corn
2 cups milk
Salt and pepper to taste
Fresh parsley for garnishing

Melt butter in soup pot.
Add onions and carrots and cook for 4-5 minutes.
Stir in flour and stir frequently for 5 minutes.
Slowly add half the clam juice, scraping the bottom of the
    pot to make sure flour mixes in.
Stir in remaining broth and bring to a boil.
Add potatoes, corn, and milk, simmer, stirring 30 minutes.
Add the chopped clams, salt, pepper, simmer for 5 minutes.
Heat thoroughly. Garnish with parsley (optional).
Serves 4-5

# Shrimp Bisque

2 pounds raw shrimp, cleaned and deveined
3 Tablespoon butter
2 tablespoon carrots, minced
2 Tablespoon  onion, minced
2 Tablespoon celery, minced
1-2 cloves garlic,  minced
1 bay leaf
½ teaspoon thyme
3 Tablespoons parsley, minced
1 Tablespoon lemon juice (fresh is best)
2 cups chicken stock
1 cup fish stock*
1 cup half and half cream
½ cup heavy cream
Salt and pepper to taste
Tabasco
Worcestershire sauce
½ cup dry white wine**
Minced dill

Mince 1 ½ pounds of shrimp and set  aside.
Melt butter and saute the rest of the shrimp with carrot,
    onion, celery and garlic for about 6-8 minutes.
Remove shrimp, dice and reserve.
Combine minced raw shrimp, bay leaf, thyme, parsley,
    lemon juice and stocks.
Cover, bring to boil, simmer for 45 minutes, stirring.
Discard bay leaf.  Puree mixture in blender or immerse blender.
Reheat with creams and reserved shrimp.
Add seasonings to taste, Tabasco and Worcestershire sauce.
Before serving, add wine.
Heat for 3 minutes.
Sprinkle with dill.
Serves 4-6

*You can use 3 cups of chicken stock or find fish or clam juice in the store.

* *Always use wine that you would drink.

Shrimp Bisque © Connie Hope

# Crab Chowder

4 slices bacon, diced
2 Tablespoons flour
3 cups milk (you can use half milk and half light cream)
1 Tablespoon onion juice
1 cup tomato juice (I use Clamato)
¼ teaspoon basil
¼ teaspoon marjoram
¼ garlic powder
Salt and pepper to taste
1 cup potatoes, diced and cooked
2 cups flaked crab meat
Paprika
Lemon slice

Saute bacon until crisp. Remove, put on paper towel to drain.
Save about 1 ½-2 Tablespoons of fat.
Sprinkle with flour and cook, stirring continually.
Gradually add milk. Stir, cook until smooth and thickened.
Add onion juice, tomato juice and seasonings.
Simmer covered for about 10 minutes.
Add potatoes and crab, reheat. Add salt and pepper to taste.
Sprinkle with paprika and lemon slice.
Serves 4-5

# Clam Chowder

1 cup minced green onions (or you can use leeks)
1-2 cloves garlic, minced
¼ pound diced salt pork
3 Tablespoons butter
3 cups chicken broth
2 ½ cups potatoes, diced
1 bay leaf
¼ teaspoon thyme
1/8 teaspoon allspice
Salt and pepper to taste
3 dozen clams, shucked and reserve juice*
1 cup bottled clam juice
1 ½ cups half and half cream
½ cup heavy cream
Green onions, chopped for garnish
Butter pieces

Saute onion, garlic and salt pork in butter until soft.
Add broth, potatoes, bay leaf, spices, salt, pepper, and
    minced clams, add to soup with juices and creams. Reheat.
Stir in butter pieces, sprinkle with paprika and green onions.
Serves 6.

This is a quick cook for the Crab Chowder.

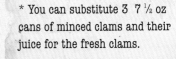

* You can substitute 3  7 ½ oz cans of minced clams and their juice for the fresh clams.

Can be served as a lunch or use as a main dish for dinner.

Use a nice crusty roll or bread

# Crab and Corn Bisque

1 Tablespoon olive oil
1 small onion, finely chopped
1 small red pepper, finely chopped
2 celery stalks, finely chopped
2-4 cloves garlic, minced
2 Tablespoons flour
1 cup low sodium tomato juice (can use Clamato)
2 cups fat-free seafood, chicken or vegetable broth
1 Tablespoon lemon juice
4 cups corn kernels  (canned or frozen)
2 cups low fat milk
1 pound lump crabmeat drained, cans
Salt and pepper to taste

Garnish:
3 Tablespoons chopped fresh basil
Medium tomato, seeded and finely diced
1 avocado, chopped
2 teaspoons fresh lime juice
1 teaspoon virgin olive oil
Salt and pepper to taste

Heat oil in large stock pot.
Add onion, pepper, celery, and garlic, and cook 5-7 minutes.
Add flour and cook until blended, about 2-3 minutes.
Add tomato juice, broth, lemon juice, and corn to the pot.
Stir  continuously for 10-15 minutes or until corn is tender.
Reduce heat and add milk and crab.
Stir carefully to combine, then heat 4-5 minutes.
Season with salt and pepper.
Put garnish in a small bowl. Toss and set aside.
Put soup in bowls and top with garnish and serve.
Serves 6

# Seafood Chowder

8 slices bacon, chopped
2 medium onions, chopped
1 ½ cups celery, chopped
2 teaspoons dried thyme
2 bay leaves
4 cups bottled clam juice
2 cups fish stock
2 potatoes, peeled and diced
1 pound shrimp, fresh or frozen deveined and shelled
2 pounds clams
1 pound cod, boneless and pound of scallops cut in chunks
2 Tablespoons butter
1 cup heavy cream
Salt and pepper to taste
1/8 teaspoon cayenne pepper

Saute bacon in soup pot, 5 minutes. Drain on paper towel.
Add onion, celery, bay leaf and thyme, saute medium heat.
Add clam juice, fish stock and potatoes, bring to a boil.
Simmer until potatoes are tender about 20 minutes.
Add cream and ½ bacon, simmer 5 minutes. Set aside
In a skillet, melt butter, saute scallops 3-4 minutes.
Add all seafood, salt, pepper, cayenne pepper to soup.
Garnish with bacon.
Serves 4-6

This makes a really large amount of chowder. Have lots of friends over.

# Seafood Chowder-Variation

4 cups water or broth (fish broth, clam juice or combination)
2 large onions, diced
3 carrots, sliced ¼ inch
7 potatoes, peeled and cubed
1 pound salmon, cod, scallops, cut into chunks
1 pound shrimp, peeled and deveined
1 (6 oz) can crabmeat, drained and flaked
6 oz cooked lobster meat, shredded
2 (6.5 oz) cans chopped clams, drained
4 ¼ cup heavy whipping cream
2 cups half and half
1 ½ cups butter, cut into chunks
Salt and pepper to taste

In a soup pot, add water or juice. Add onions, carrots, cook
 10 minutes until tender. Add potatoes, cook 15-20 minutes.
Stir in all fish except clams and cook 10-15 minutes.
Drain half of liquid, add clams, heavy cream, half and half.
Place butter chunks atop of soup.  Salt, pepper.
Cover simmer, until fish is flaky, 30 minutes.
Serves 4-6

Conch Chowder is as much a part of the Florida heritage as the old clam chowder is of New England heritage. However, Conch Chowder is closer to the Manhattan clam chowder, which is a tomato-based rather than the cream like New England Clam Chowder. One of the many Conch Chowder legends stated that the soup originated with Bahamian fishermen who had settled in Key West in the 19th century.

The Conch is a giant edible sea snail. It has been used in Caribbean and Native Indian diets. The Indians used the shells to make axes, scrapers, fishhooks, jewelry, and musical instruments. These spiraled shellfish are found as far north as Bermuda and as far south as Brazil. Key West's staple diet was at one time made up of the Conch.

Some of the other popular Conch dishes found in the Florida area are conch fritters, conch salad, and conch stew. It is high in protein and low in fat. Please, when you are in Florida, make an effort to at least sample the famous Conch.

# Conch Chowder

1 pound conch, trimmed *
3 to 4 fresh limes, juiced (or more)
5-6 Tablespoons tomato paste (I use the tube of paste)
4 strips bacon, cooked crispy and cut in ½ inch strips
3 Tablespoons olive oil
1 onion, finely chopped
1 carrot, finely chopped
3 ribs celery, finely chopped
3-4 cloves garlic, finely chopped
1 green bell pepper, finely chopped
1 Jalapeno pepper, seeded and minced (use gloves)
3 large ripe tomatoes, peeled, seeded and finely chopped
¼ cup dark rum
¼ cup dry sherry
1 ½ pound potatoes, peeled and diced
2 bay leaves
1 teaspoon dried thyme
½ cup parsley, finely chopped
8 cups water
1 Tablespoon Worcestershire sauce
1 teaspoon Tabasco sauce
Salt and pepper to taste

Tenderize the conch by pounding with a meat mallet for a few minutes.
Cut the conch into 1 inch pieces, chop in a food processor.
Mix with the conch, 2 Tablespoons lime and tomato paste.
Set aside.
Make sure bacon is drained of fat.
In a soup pot, add the olive oil, onion, carrot, celery, garlic bell pepper and Jalapeno pepper.
Cook until lightly browned about 6-7 minutes, medium heat.
Add tomatoes and heat for 2 -4 minutes.
Stir in the rum, sherry and bring to a boil.
Stir in the potatoes, conch mixture, bay leaves, thyme, parsley, water, Worcestershire sauce, Tabasco sauce, and salt and pepper.
Bring to a boil, then reduce to a simmer and cook until the potatoes are tender (about 1 hour).
Before serving, discard the 2 bay leaves.
Serve hot.
Serves 6-8

*To prepare the conch for cooking: Trim off any bits of dark membrane. Place in a Ziploc bag and pound it with a meat mallet to a thickness of about ¼ inch. The conch should be then ground in a food processor.

# Conch Chowder

1/8 pound salt pork, chopped fine
2 onions, finely chopped
1 bell pepper, green or other colors, chopped fine
1 Hot pepper, remove seeds, veins, and chop*
12 oz conch meat, or if you can't find that, use clam
3 cups canned tomatoes, chopped
2 cups canned potatoes, diced
2 cups tomato juice
½ cup tomato puree
½ tablespoon thyme
Salt and pepper to taste
1-2 bay leaves crushed

Saute pork in a large soup pot.
Remove and set aside.
Add onions, bell peppers and saute.
Add the hot pepper.
Add the pork, conch, tomatoes, potatoes, puree, and thyme.
Add tomato juice as needed.
Bring to a slow boil for 15 minutes.
Simmer for 45 minutes.
Serves 6

# Conch Chowder (not as spicy)

3 onions, finely chopped
3-4 cloves of garlic, minced
1 green bell pepper, finely chopped
1 (14 ½ oz) can whole tomatoes, cut up
2 ½ to 3 pounds conch meat, cleaned and chopped,
2 potatoes, peeled and finely chopped
2 quarts water
Salt and pepper to taste.

In a large soup pot over medium heat, add the onion, garlic,
    bell peppers and tomatoes.
Cook until vegetables are soft.
Reduce heat to low and add conch, potatoes and enough
    water to make it soupy, but not too much water.
Let simmer for 1 hour. Salt and pepper to taste.
Serves 6

*There are several types of hot peppers that can be used. I use them sparingly as I don't like things too 'Hot'.

Make sure you clean the veins and seeds out which makes them less 'Hot'.

See Appendix for Details

Serrano Pepper

Jalapeno Pepper

# Halibut and Shellfish Soup

1 teaspoon olive oil
2 shallots, chopped
2 cloves of garlic, minced
2 medium tomatoes, diced (or use canned tomatoes and dice)
4 oz dry white wine
1 cup clam juice
2 cups vegetable broth
¾ pound halibut filet, skin removed, cut into pieces
1 pound shrimp, peeled, deveined (best fresh)
1 dozen littleneck clams, clean shells
Pinch of saffron
1 teaspoon fresh thyme
¼ cup fresh chopped parsley
Crusty bread

Add olive oil; saute shallots, and garlic, slowly 5 minutes.
Add tomatoes, wine, clam juice, broth, saffron, fresh thyme.
Stir and simmer for 15 minutes.
Add clams, cook 2-4 minutes, discard any that did not open.
Add shrimp and fish, simmer for 5-7 minutes.
Shrimp should be pink. Serve with crusty bread.
Serves 4-6.

# Fresh Salmon Chowder

3 Tablespoons butter
½ cup celery, diced
½ cup carrot, diced
¼ cup onion, finely chopped
2 Tablespoons flour
1 2/3 cups fish broth or use chicken broth
2 cups potatoes, diced
12 to 16 oz fresh salmon or canned flaked salmon, diced
1 cup peas, canned or frozen
2 cups half and half or whole milk
2 cups Cheddar cheese, shredded
1 Tablespoon parsley, fresh chopped
Salt and pepper to taste
Serve with oyster cracker

Heat butter, add celery, carrot, and onion saute 5-7 minutes.
Stir in flour, blend well. Stir in broth and add potatoes.
Bring to a simmer, stirring frequently.
Cover, simmer for 18-20 minutes or until potatoes are tender.
Add salmon and peas and simmer for 8-10 minutes.
Salmon should be flaky. Add half and half, cheese and parsley. Cook until cheese is melted. Salt and pepper.
Serves 5-6

# Connie's Cooking Tips

Garlic—Garlic is widely used around the world for its pungent flavor as a seasoning and condiment. For centuries it has been said that garlic has many health benefits. Bulbs of garlic were found in the tombs of Egyptians and was even mentioned in the Bible. Recently many studies have been conducted with some positive results. But always consult your doctor before considering using any herb as a medicine. I have done some research and found some of these items.

Here are some of the stated benefits:

1. Garlic tends to reduce the frequency of colds and flu or helps with infections.
2. Helps reduce cholesterol.
3. Helps reduce fat in the body. Luke warm water, I lemon squeezed with 2 cloves of raw garlic.
4. Reduces the risk of some cancers. It can help prevent cancer compounds from forming and developing into tumors.
5. Spread garlic cloves on insect bite to reduce pain and reduce the poison.
6. Regular taking of garlic is said to help reduce the risk of heart attacks.
7. Stops vampires in their tracks…..Just seeing if you were reading this.
8. Always consult your doctors before using garlic for any of these benefits.

Tip:

Removing the paper skin of the garlic clove:
Separate into several cloves.
Place the cloves on a paper towel.
Heat in microwave for 20 to 30 seconds depending on the number of cloves.
Be careful—it's hot when you take it out.
The paper skin will peel off.
Then mince into small pieces.

Research done on:
Webmed.com
Wikipedia.com

The beans that are in the bag of 15 bean soup:

Northern
Pinto
Large Lima
Black eye peas
Garbanzo
Baby Lima
Green split peas
Kidney
Cranberry
Small white
Pink Beans
Small red
Yellow split pea
Lentil
Navy
White kidney
Black beans

Just remember—Soup is always better the next day.

*Squeeze container of spices

* * If you don't have time to soak overnight, put in a soup pot, fill to cover beans, and heat over medium for 40-50 minutes. Bring to a slow boil, rinse and drain. Then put the ingredients together.

# 15 Bean Soup with Ham  (Bag of Beans)
# (Also see Crock Pots Bean Soup)

1 20 oz Bag of Beans
1 cup onion, chopped
1 (14.5  oz) can of tomatoes, diced
1 teaspoon chili powder
1 lemon, cut and juiced
2-3 cloves of garlic, minced
1 cup of ham, cubed (If you have a ham bone, add that also)
8 cups of water
2 Tablespoons 'Better than Bouillon-Ham'
½ teaspoon lemongrass—use the squeeze containers *
½ teaspoon basil (dried or in the squeeze container)
Salt and pepper to taste

Soak beans over night in enough water to cover them.
Rinse and drain the next morning.**
Put 2 cups of water in a measuring cup and add 2
    Tablespoons of 'Better than Bouillon Ham' and heat for
    3-4 minute in the microwave.
Place beans in the large soup pot with the 6 cups of water
    that you have added the Bouillon mix to.
Add onions, ham cubes, and garlic.
Bring to a boil, reduce heat and simmer covered for 1 hour.
Stir. Add tomatoes, chili powder, lemon, lemongrass and basil.
Simmer for another hour.
Serves 6-8

# Ham and Potato Soup

2 cups cauliflower florets
2 Tablespoons water
4 oz ham, chopped in cubes (about ¾ cup)
2 teaspoons olive oil
1 onion, diced
1 carrot, diced
1 cup celery, diced
1 cup red pepper, chopped
2-3 cloves of garlic, minced
8 oz red potatoes, cut into ½ inch cubes (or use any potato)
4 cups chicken broth
$\frac{1}{8}$ teaspoon crushed red pepper
½ teaspoon thyme

In a soup pot, heat oil, stir in cauliflower, carrot, celery, red
    pepper, ham, garlic, cook 6 minutes, until  are tender.
Stir in flour, cook for 4 minutes, stir continuously.
Stir in chicken broth, 1 cup at a time.
Bring to boil, then simmer for 15 minutes, stir occasionally.
Stir in potatoes and cook for 15-20 minutes or until tender.
Salt, pepper, red pepper and thyme.  Heat 10 minutes.
Take out a few small potatoes, put in a bowl and mash.
Return to pot and mix. This will thicken the soup.
Serve 5-6.

# Ham and Wild Rice Chowder

½ cup onion, chopped
¼ cup butter, cubed
2-3 cloves of garlic, minced
6 Tablespoons flour
Salt and pepper to taste
4 cups of chicken broth
1 ½ cups potatoes, peeled and cubed
½ cup carrots, chopped
1 bay leaf
½ teaspoon dried thyme
¼ teaspoons ground nutmeg
3 cups wild rice, cooked
1 ½ cups cooked ham, cubed
2 cups half and half
1 (15 ¼ oz) can corn, drained
Fresh parsley or cilantro, tips for garnishing

In a soup pot, saute onion in butter until tender.
Add garlic and cook medium heat 2-3 minutes.
Stir flour, salt and pepper until blended. Add broth gradually.
Bring to a boil and stir for 3 minutes to thicken.
Add potatoes, carrots, bay leaf, thyme, nutmeg, boil.
Reduce heat, simmer 30-35 minutes until tender.
Serves 4-5.

Variation:
Instead of olive oil use 2 slices bacon,
heated until soft then chopped.
Use drippings to heat veggies.

Variations:

½ teaspoon dried
     rosemary
1 carrot, chopped

Stir in rice, ham, cream, and corn;
do not boil, heat to warm.
Remove bay leaf and garnish with
parsley or cilantro.
Serves 4-5.

# Ham and Corn Chowder

1 can chicken broth
12 oz evaporated skim milk
2 cups whole kernel corn (frozen or canned)
½ cup ham, chopped
4 green onions, chopped
¼ cup red pepper flakes
½ cup instant mashed potato flakes
Salt and pepper to taste

In a medium soup pot, add chicken broth and milk.
Add corn, ham, onions and pepper flakes.
Bring to a boil, stirring continually.
Reduce to simmer, add instant mashed potato flakes, stir.
Cover, simmer 10 minutes or until veggies are soft.
Salt and pepper.
Serves 3-4

# Cheesy Ham Chowder

10 strips of bacon, diced
1 large onion, diced
1 cup carrots, diced
3 Tablespoons flour
3 cups milk
1 ½ cups water
2 ½ cups potatoes, cubed
1 (15 ¼ oz) can whole kernel corn, drained
2 teaspoons chicken bouillon or use 'Better than Bouillon'
Salt and pepper to taste
3 cups shredded cheddar cheese
2 cups ham, cubed

Cook bacon over medium heat until crispy.
Use a slotted spoon, remove bacon to a paper towel.
In drippings, saute onion and carrots until tender.
Stir in flour until smooth. Gradually add milk and water.
Bring to a boil and stir for 2-3 minutes.
Add potatoes, corn, bouillon, salt and pepper.
Reduce heat, simmer 25-30 minutes, potatoes to be tender.
Add cheese and ham, heat until cheese is melted, ham is hot.
Stir in bacon.
Serves 8

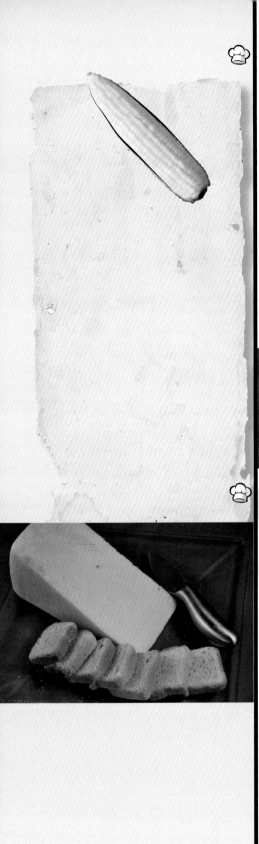

# Connie's Cooking Tips

## Onion Tips

1. Cooking onions using high heat makes the onion bitter. When sautéing onions, use low to medium heat.

2. Prepare onion close to the cooking and serving time. The flavor diminishes with time.

3. Yellow onions make up about 88% of the market. They are full flavored and a standby in most cooking. Yellow onions turn rich, dark brown when cooked and give French Onion soup its tangy sweet flavor.

4. Red Onion have a wonderful color and are great in grilling. They account for about 7 % of the market.

5. The white onion holds about 5% of the market. White onions are used in classic Mexican Cuisine. They are golden in color and sweet when sautéed.

6. What makes you cry…in an onion?
   Onions contain complex sulphur compounds. When you cut into an onion, two chemical reactions take place. First, your knife cuts through the cells of the onion; its enzymes release a strong odor. Second, the onion releases allicon, a volatile sulfur gas that irritates your eyes. This makes your eyes tear to get rid of the irritation.

7. To stop from crying, do not cut the root end (the flattened end) of the onion until the very end. Or cut the onion under running water or submerge onion in a bowl. Or put the onion in the refrigerator for a time, then cut it.

8. To select your husband-to-be from among several suitors, it is said, that if the name of each suitor is written on an onion and then placed in a cool, dark place, the first onion that sprouts will be the man you should marry. Does this method work better than Match.com?

9. The bigger and firmer the onion, the easier it is to cut. A wet onion is easier to peel than a dry one. A cool onion is easier to cut than a room temperature one.

10. Sweet onions are higher in water and sugar content, so they require more care in storing. Treat them gently to avoid bruising. Sweet onions should be wrapped lightly in a plastic bag, then put in a second bag and refrigerated.

The Vidalia onion is my favorite, but it is seasonal.

# Minestrone Soup

Minestrone Soup is an Italian soup that includes vegetables, pasta, beans, and some-times meat.* It is a very versatile soup. You can add what vegetables, beans and pasta you like. I love mine with carrots, celery, zucchini, tomatoes, and green beans. You can also use cannellini beans or navy beans, which are white and kidney beans, which are red. Any small pasta will work: ditalini, small shell, elbow macaroni or any other. Garnish the soup bowl with parmesan cheese. Serve with crusty bread.

2 Tablespoons olive oil
1 yellow onion, chopped
2-3 cloves garlic, minced
1 carrot peeled and diced
1 stalk celery, diced
1 zucchini, diced
1 cup green beans-frozen or fresh **( or any type bean)
2 (14 oz) can diced tomatoes
6 cups vegetable broth (can use chicken or half and half)
1 can each kidney beans and cannellini, rinsed and drained
1 cup pasta—any type of small pasta
½ teaspoon dried oregano
1 teaspoon dried basil
½ teaspoon rosemary
Salt and pepper to taste
Garnish with Parmesan cheese

Heat oil in soup pot; add onion, garlic, carrot, celery.
Cook 5-6 minutes until onions are translucent.
Add zucchini, green beans and diced tomatoes.
Cook for 5 minutes. Add broth, beans, pasta, oregano,
    rosemary and basil.
Simmer until vegetables and pasta are tender about 15-20
    minutes. Salt and pepper to taste. Garnish with
    parmesan cheese.
Serves 6-8

*If you want to add a meat. Add ½ pound ground beef, cooked and drained
  Or
  1 pound of sausage removed from casing
  and fried and drained.

** I use the juice from the green beans in the soup. Adds to the flavor.

I really like light or dark kidney beans in this soup.
¼ to 1 cup drained and rinsed.

Options:
Use beef or chicken broth instead of vegetable broth.

Add:
2 cups diced peeled potatoes
Or
2 cups shredded cabbage
Or
1cup fresh spinach
Or
1 cup fresh Swiss chard
Or
1 can lima beans

Instead of olive oil, substitute 2 slices bacon chopped.

Minestrone Soup  © Connie Hope

# Zucchini Soup

1 ½ pounds of zucchini
3 Tablespoons butter or margarine
1 small onion, chopped
1 teaspoon thyme
6 cups chicken broth
½ cup white rice, uncooked
Salt and pepper to taste
Grated parmesan cheese for top

Clean and cut off ends of zucchini and grate.
In a large pot, melt butter and add onions.
Then add zucchini and thyme, heat for a few minutes.
Add broth and rice and bring to a boil.
Reduce heat and simmer for 30 minutes, puree with blender.
Serve with Parmesan cheese on top.
Serves 4-6

# Zucchini Soup (served Hot or Cold)

2 Tablespoons margarine
2 onions, chopped
2 Russet potatoes, peeled and diced
8 zucchini , chopped
¼ teaspoon dried thyme ( fresh is ½ teaspoon)
¼ teaspoon dried rosemary ( fresh is ½ teaspoon)
½ teaspoon dried basil (fresh is ¾ teaspoon)
Salt and pepper to taste
4 cups chicken broth ( or substitute vegetable broth)
1 cup milk (or use soy milk)
1 Tablespoon soy sauce
4 Tablespoons dill, chopped

In a fry pan, melt margarine. Add onion, cook until
    translucent.  Add potatoes, zucchini and spices.
Simmer for 5-8 minutes. Put in soup pot, add broth.
Bring to a boil. Add zucchini mix, simmer for 15 minutes.
Put in a food processor and blend until smooth.
Return to pot and add milk and bring almost to a boil.
Add soy sauce, stir. Serve cold or hot.
Serves  4-6

This is great with a grilled cheese sandwich on a cold day.  (Or if you are like me, I can have soup on a cold or a hot day.  I love it!)

You can use a combination of yellow zucchini and green zucchini squash to make up a total of about 8 zucchini.

Just a little different, but you can serve either one hot or cold.   Your choice.

For thickener in any soup, you can use instant potato mix.  About ¼ or 1/3 cup.  It will change the taste to more potato taste, but it will add thickness.

Immersion Blender

# Zucchini and Fennel Soup

1 large fennel bulb, 8 small fronds reserved for
  garnishing. Cored and slice in ½ inch thickness
2 Tablespoons fresh lemon juice
2 Tablespoons olive oil
1 ¾ pounds of zucchini, sliced and chopped into
  chunks
1 large yellow onion, thinly sliced
1 clove garlic, minced (I have put more in the soup)
4 cups chicken stock
Salt and pepper to taste
½ cup sour cream for garnishing

In a medium pot, cover the pieces of fennel with water. Add
  lemon juice.  Bring to a boil.
Cover and simmer over lower heat until fennel is
  tender, about 20-25 minutes.
Drain the fennel.
In a soup pot, heat oil and add zucchini, onion, garlic.
Cook over medium heat. Stir occasionally until
  softened, 15 minutes.
Add chicken stock and cooked fennel and bring to a
  boil.
Cover and simmer medium heat until vegetables are
  softened, about 10 minutes.
Puree the soup in food processor or immersion blender.
Return to pot and season with salt and pepper.
Put in soup bowl and put a dollop of sour cream on
  each soup bowl and a fennel frond.
Serves 4-6

# Creamy Zucchini Soup

1 Tablespoon butter or margarine
2 Tablespoons olive oil
1 large onion, chopped
1 ½ pounds of zucchini, cleaned and chopped
½ package (14 oz) firm tofu, cubed
1 teaspoon red pepper flakes
1 teaspoon dried oregano
3 cups vegetable broth
½ cup cottage cheese
Salt and pepper to taste

Melt butter and heat oil in a large skillet.

Add onions and cook for 5-6 minutes or until onions are
    translucent.

Mix in chopped zucchini and tofu.

Add red pepper flakes and oregano.

Continue cooking and stirring for 10-12 minutes or until
    zucchini is tender.

In a soup pot, add vegetable broth and bring to a boil.

Reduce heat and add the zucchini mixture.

Simmer for 40 minutes.

Add the cottage cheese.

In a blender or an immersion blender, puree soup mixture.

Serve hot or chilled.

Serves 4-5.

Creamy Zucchini Soup © Connie Hope

# Cauliflower Chowder (It's really a soup)

1 head cauliflower, cut in florets
3 Tablespoons butter
½ cup onions, minced
1-2 cloves of garlic, minced
2/3 cup rice
Salt and pepper to taste
5 cups chicken broth
2/3 cup Parmesan cheese, grated
2 Tablespoons parsley, cut or minced

In a large soup pot, melt butter, saute onion until transparent.
Stir in garlic and saute.
Stir in rice and coat with butter. Salt and pepper to taste.
Add broth and cauliflower.
Cover and simmer 10-12 minutes until cauliflower is tender.
Sprinkle with cheese and parsley.
Serves 4

# Mushroom and Potato Chowder

Use your favorite mushrooms for this soup.
I like Portabella, but you can use any of them.

You can use chicken broth, or use 'Better than Bouillon' paste in mushroom.

You can even puree this soup. I like it a little chunky. Your choice.

½ cup onions, chopped
¼ cup butter
2 Tablespoons flour
Salt and pepper to taste
3 cups water (or mushroom flavoring)
1 can cream of mushroom soup
1 pound mushrooms, sliced thin—any kind
1 cup celery, chopped
1 ½ cups potatoes, diced (I like new potatoes)
½ cup carrots, chopped
½ teaspoon basil (or you can use thyme)
1 cup half and half cream
¼ Parmesan cheese, grated (I also like Gruyere instead)

In a large soup pot, saute onion in butter until tender.
Add flour, salt and pepper. Stir to make a paste.
Gradually add the water, and soup, stir constantly.
Bring to a boil for 1 minute, stirring constantly.
Add mushrooms, celery, potatoes and carrots.
Reduce heat, cover and simmer for 30-40 minutes.
Add cream, and parmesan cheese, heat 5 minutes.
Serves 4

# Asparagus Soup

1 cup yellow onion, chopped
6 green onions, sliced
3 Tablespoons butter or margarine
1 ½ - 2 cups fresh mushrooms, sliced
1 pound fresh asparagus, cut into 1 inch pieces
1  49 ½ oz box of chicken or vegetable broth
½ cup fresh parsley, chopped
Salt and pepper to taste
½ teaspoon dried thyme (use more if fresh thyme, about 1
    Tablespoon)
1/8 teaspoon cayenne pepper—optional
2 cups cooked rice
3 Tablespoons cornstarch--optional
1/2 cup water--optional

In large soup pot, saute onion in margarine or butter for 3-4
    minutes or until translucent.
Add mushrooms and cook until tender.
Add asparagus, broth, and seasoning.
Cover and simmer for 30-40 minutes. Add rice.
To thicken, combine water and cornstarch with wire whisk.
Bring to a boil, lower heat and stir for 3 minutes to thicken.
Serves 6-8

# Cream of Asparagus Soup

¼ cup margarine or butter
1 onion, chopped
3-4 stalks celery, chopped
3 Tablespoons flour
5 cups water (you can use vegetable broth or chicken broth)
4 Tablespoons chicken bouillon powder
1 potato, peeled and diced
1 pound fresh asparagus, trimmed and chopped
1 cup half and half
1 Tablespoon soy sauce
Salt and pepper to taste

Melt margarine in soup pot.
Add onions, celery, and saute until tender about 45 minutes.
Stir in flour and mix.
Cook for 1-2 minutes stirring constantly.
Add water or chicken broth, and soup base.
Stir to make sure smooth and bring to a boil.
Add potatoes, asparagus. Reduce, simmer for 20 minutes.
Puree in food processor or immersion blender.
Return to pot and heat.
Stir in half and half cream, soy sauce.
Serves 4-5

I like to use Vidalia onions as they
are sweeter.

Variation:

• Add 4 Tablespoons dry vermouth.

• Add 2 Tablespoons lemon juice

• 5 Sprigs fresh thyme

• 3 cloves garlic, minced

Herbs to add:

1 Tablespoon curry powder
Or ¼ cup parsley, chopped
Or ¼ cup fresh dill
Or ¼ cup tarragon
Or ½ cup cilantro,
    chopped

Or Dill pesto for topping

Dill Pesto

1/2 cup fresh dill
½ cup parsley
1 clove garlic
1 Tablespoon pine nuts
1 Tablespoon olive oil
1 Tablespoon parmesan cheese

Puree in food processor
or immersion blender.
Slowly add olive oil.

* Details found in Wikipedia on the internet
** Details found in Wikipedia on the internet

Carrots and carrot juice are a great source of vitamin, C, D, E, K, B and B6. They contain antioxidants, dietary fiber and minerals, help clean your arteries and protect from free radicals. It is thought that Beta carotene helps in the fight against some cancers. On the other hand, my mother used to tell me if I ate my carrots it would help my eyesight …please, mom. *    Little did I realize that the lack of vitamin A can cause poor vision; adding more carrots to your diet can help this situation. Wow, you were correct, mom.**

# Carrot Soup  Basic

1 Tablespoon olive oil
2-3 cloves of garlic, minced
1 large sweet onion, chopped fine
4 cups vegetable broth ( or you can use chicken)
1 ½ pounds carrots, (about 3 cups) cleaned, cut into ½ inch
    section
Juice of ½ lemon
Salt and pepper to taste
Pinch of sugar
Parsley sprig for topping

Heat oil in large soup pot.
Add garlic and onions and saute for 3 minutes or until
    onions are translucent.
Add broth and carrots, bring to a boil.
Lower heat and simmer for 30-40 minutes or until carrots
    are tender.
Puree the mix in a food processor or immersion blender.
You can make it very smooth or let it be a little chunky—
    your choice.
Add lemon juice, pinch of sugar, salt and pepper to taste.
Serve with parsley sprigs or croutons on top.
Serves 4-5

Carrot Soup pureed © Connie Hope

# Carrot Soup

topped with whipped cream and dill

1 Tablespoon olive oil
1 large yellow onion, chopped
2 pounds carrots, cut into ½ inch sections
4 cups chicken broth or vegetable broth
1 Tablespoon grated ginger
Salt and pepper to taste
½ cup heavy cream
3 Tablespoons chopped fresh dill.

Heat oil in large soup pot.

Add onion and cook until soft about 4 minutes.

Add carrots, broth, ginger, salt and pepper

Boil, then lower and simmer. Puree in blender or immersion
   blender until smooth. Return to pot and warm.

Wire whisk the cream and dill until they form peaks.

Serve with a dollop of cream or dill on top.

Serves 4-5

# Cream of Carrot Soup

1 ½ pound of carrots, sliced ¼ inch round (about 3 cups)
1 stalk celery, chopped
3-3 ½ cups leeks, chopped finely
1 bay leaf
¼ cup fresh parsley sprigs, chopped
6 cups chicken broth (or you can use vegetable broth)
1 cup heavy cream
1/8 teaspoon nutmeg
Salt and pepper to taste

In a large soup pot, add 3 cups broth and cook carrots,
   celery, leeks, bay leaf and parsley 15- 20 minutes.

Removed bay leaf.

Puree in blender or immersion blender and return to pot.

Add remaining broth, cream and seasonings.

Simmer 15-20 minutes. Serve with croutons.

Serves 5-6

Can be vegan if you eliminate the heavy cream, and add ½ cup vegetable broth.

Variation:
Add 2 parsnips, peeled and chopped.

# Carrot Soup with an Indian Flair

1 Tablespoon olive oil
3 ½ cups carrots cut in ¼ inch pieces
1 onion, chopped
1 teaspoon coriander seeds *
1 teaspoon mustard seeds*
1 teaspoon cumin seeds*
1 Tablespoon fresh ginger, peeled and minced
Salt and pepper to taste
4 cup vegetable broth
1 teaspoon crushed red pepper
2 teaspoons grated lime peel
2 teaspoons lime juice
Yogurt for garnish

Grate the coriander, mustard and cumin seeds in a spice mill.*
In a soup pot, heat oil and add the spices for just a minute.
Add onion, carrots, ginger, and lime peel and simmer for 2-3 minutes.
Add vegetable broth and red pepper and simmer until carrots are tender about 30 minutes.
Put ½ mix in blender, then the other half, or use an immersion blender and blend until smooth.
Return to pot and add more broth if too thick.
Stir in lime juice, salt and pepper.
Garnish with yogurt.
Serves 6-8

Carrot Soup with an Indian Flair © Connie Hope

# Bean Soup—Basic

1 pound beans—soaked overnight in water
9 cups chicken broth, vegetable broth or half and half
  water and broth.
Ham bone with a little bit of meat left on it
2 Tablespoons ketchup or spaghetti sauce
Salt and pepper to taste
1-2 Tablespoons of cornstarch for thickening

Drain beans, put in large pot with broth, ham bone, salt and pepper.
Cover and simmer for 2 plus hours over medium heat  Do Not Boil.
Remove ham bone and put the smaller pieces of ham from
  the bone back into the soup.
Add ketchup or spaghetti sauce for color.
If too thin, add the cornstarch for thickener and stir.

Variation: All of these can be added or choose the ones you like.

1 cup of celery, diced
1 cup of carrots, diced
1 cup onion, diced
3 medium potatoes-quartered and diced
1 can tomatoes, diced
1 cup green beans, canned or frozen
½ cup parsley, chopped
1-2 clove of garlic, chopped

# White Bean Soup

1 pound dried white cannellini beans
4 cups yellow onions, sliced thin (about 3 onions)
¼ cup olive oil
2-3 cloves of garlic, minced
1 large fresh rosemary branch
8 cups chicken stock
1 bay leaf
Salt and pepper to taste

Soak beans at least 6 hours or overnight.
In a large pot, add oil and sauté onions until translucent. 15 minutes.
Add the garlic and cook 3-4 minutes.
Drain the beans and add to pot.
Add stock, bay leaf, rosemary.  Cover and bring to a boil.
Then reduce heat to a simmer for 40 minutes. Beans should be soft.
Remove the rosemary and bay leaf.
Either put the soup in a food processor and puree so it will be smooth,
  or leave it chunky with the beans and vegetables whole.

This basic recipe has no vegetables, herbs or spices.  The variations can add much more flavor to the basic bean soup.

There are as many Bean soup recipes as there are different types of beans. You can use any type bean you enjoy or maybe experiment using several types. I will include several examples of bean soup and list many other variations you can experiment with.  Maybe you have your favorite herbs you can add for your own personal taste.

I always think any type of bean soup is better the second day.  It has thickened and the flavors mingle and deepens the taste.

# White Bean and Sausage Soup

2 Tablespoons olive oil
1 ½ pounds sweet or medium Italian sausage, sliced
2 oz prosciutto ham, thinly sliced and minced
1 large onion, diced
2 carrots, peeled and diced
2 medium stalks of celery, diced
1 teaspoon dried thyme
3 (15.8 oz) cans of Great Northern or Navy beans, rinsed and drained
4 cups chicken broth

Heat oil in a soup pot. Add sausages and cook until browned.
Remove and put on paper towel.
Add prosciutto, onion, carrots, celery, thyme. Stir, 8 minutes.
In a bowl, mash one can of beans with a fork.
Add broth, whole and mashed beans, sausage to mix.
Cover and simmer for 30 minutes.
Serves 4-5.

White Bean and Sausage Soup © Connie Hope

# White Bean and Leek Soup

4 cups cooked white beans (Cannellini, or navy)
2-3 cloves garlic, minced
3 cups leeks, thinly sliced
1 Tablespoon butter
2 cups vegetable broth
½ teaspoon thyme
¼ teaspoon rosemary
Salt and pepper to taste

In a soup pot, heat oil and add leeks, saute until soft.
Add the remaining ingredients and stir occasionally.
Bring to a boil and simmer for 15 minutes.
Remove from heat. Puree with an immerse blender.
If too thick, add additional vegetable broth.
Serves 4-5

White Bean and Leek Soup © Connie Hope

# Mushroom Barley Soup

2 Tablespoons olive oil
2 Tablespoons butter
1 yellow onion, chopped
2 stalks celery, chopped
2 carrots, peeled and chopped
½- ¾ pound fresh mushrooms, thinly sliced
10 cups mushroom broth* (or beef stock or chicken stock)
1 ¼ cups pearl barley, rinsed in cold water
1 bay leaf
Salt and pepper to taste
½ teaspoon dried rosemary
2 to 4 Tablespoons parsley, chopped for garnish

In a soup pot, warm oil and butter and saute slowly onion,
    celery, carrots until translucent about 5 minutes.
Add sliced mushrooms and cook for 4 minutes until soft.
Add broth, barley, all herbs and reserved liquid.
Bring to boil, reduce, and cook 60 minutes so barley is
    tender.
Remove bay leaf, salt and pepper to taste.
Serve in bowl with parsley as garnish.
Serve 8-10

Mushroom and Barley Soup ©Connie Hope

# Portobello Mushroom Soup

4 Portobello mushroom caps, chopped
2 Tablespoons butter or olive oil
4 cups chicken broth (or vegetable or mushroom)
1 cup half and half
4 leeks, chopped
3 Tablespoons flour

Clean mushrooms and chop in small pieces.
Butter and olive oil in pot, add leeks, saute 4-6 minutes.
Add mushrooms and saute for another 5 minutes.
Wire whisk together the flour and broth, then slowly add to
    the sautéed mix.
Bring to a boil, then reduce to a simmer.
Stir in the half and half and simmer for 10 minutes.
Serve with crusty bread.
Serves 4-6

You can add
1 teaspoon basil
Or
1 teaspoon thyme

* I use a mushroom base that really
makes a difference in the taste.
'Better than Bouillon' Mushroom
Base see appendix

If you don't use the mushroom base,
then try using this:
½ oz dried mushrooms

Soak and cover the dried mushrooms with warm water.
Soften for 30 minutes, strain mushrooms and reserve liquid.

Variation:
4 Tablespoons white wine or sherry
Instead of the half and half, use ½
cup low fat sour cream and ½ cup
fat free half and half.
Add 1 teaspoon dried parsley or
thyme.
Or kick it up a notch and add ¼ to ½
teaspoon cayenne pepper.

This, too, was my mother, Blanche's, recipe. I would stand on a chair next to her and help her cook.
What fun I had as a child. My mother, as I do, loved to make and serve soup.

Thanks, mom.

Option:
You can omit the 2 cups of half and half and use 2 cups of chicken or vegetable broth.

©Connie Hope

*You can use mushroom cubes or bouillon. Or make your own mushroom stock. Here's how:
3 cups mushrooms
8 cups water
¼ stick butter
Cook until mushrooms are tender.
Reserve liquid.

See Appendix for Better than Bouillon® and other favorites.

# Mushroom Soup with Sherry

1 pound fresh mushrooms, sliced
4 Tablespoons butter or margarine divided
½ cup onions, chopped finely
Salt and pepper to taste
3 Tablespoons flour
2 cups chicken broth (or vegetable broth)
2 Tablespoons dry sherry
2 cups half and half cream
¼ teaspoon nutmeg
parsley, chopped for garnishing

Rinse and pat dry mushrooms, sliced.
In a large skillet, melt 2 tablespoons butter and add
  mushrooms and onions, then sauté for 4-5 minutes.
Add salt and pepper and set aside.
In sauce pan melt remaining butter, stir in flour until light brown.
Remove from heat and gradually add broth.
Add sherry and heat until it starts to thicken, stirring
  constantly for 5 minutes.
Add the mushrooms and onion mixture.
Gradually add the half and half and heat until warm.
Add the nutmeg and garnish with parsley.
Serves 6-8

# Mushroom Soup

8 cups mushroom broth (chicken or vegetable)*
2 Tablespoon olive oil
2 cups mushrooms
2 large carrots, peeled and diced
2 stalks celery, diced
1 onion, finely chopped
4 large potatoes, peeled and diced
Handful of parsley, chopped
Handful of green onions, chopped
1 teaspoon dried basil
Dash of oregano and thyme
Salt and pepper to taste

Saute onion, celery and carrots for 20 minutes until caramelized.
Add mushrooms, potatoes, cook 5-10 minutes until tender.
Pour broth in, add herbs and bring to a boil.
Then simmer 10 minutes.
Puree until smooth--food processor or immersion blender.
Reheat and serve.
Serves 6-8

# Cream of Mushroom Soup

8 oz fresh mushrooms—I like the white mushrooms, sliced
2 Tablespoons onions chopped
1-2 garlic cloves, minced
2 Tablespoons butter
2-3 Tablespoons flour
2 cups chicken broth (or use vegetable broth)
1 cup light cream (or you can use 1 cup evaporated milk)
Salt and pepper to taste
¼ teaspoon nutmeg

Cut mushrooms.

Melt butter in a soup pot.

Add onions, garlic and the mushrooms.

Cook until onions are soft.

Blend in 2 Tablespoons flour, stir.

Add in broth, and heat until slightly thickened.

Add salt and pepper. Stirring continuously.

Add 1 Tablespoon of flour to cream, then add to soup.

Heat to thicken as you stir.

Serves 4-6

# Creamy Mushroom Soup

2 large onions, diced
3 Tablespoons oil
½ pound fresh mushrooms, diced
5 cups of vegetable broth or water*
Salt and pepper to taste
1-2 bay leaves
3 Tablespoons flour
2-3 Tablespoons cold water
1 Tablespoon of mushroom dried soup mix-optional
½ cup soy milk or rice milk

In a soup pot, saute onion in oil until transparent.

Add mushrooms and cook 5 minutes, stirring.

Add broth (or water), salt and pepper, bay leaves.

Cover and bring to a boil. Then simmer for 10-12 minutes.

In a bowl, dissolve flour in cold water and add to mixture.

Add mushroom soup mix if desired. Cook 7-8 minutes.

Remove bay leaves, and stir in milk.

Serves 6-8

Variation:
½ teaspoon rosemary when you add the salt and pepper.

* Or use 'Better than Bouillon' mushroom base in the water.

If you like the soup smooth, puree with an immersion blender.

*I always use a broth as it adds more flavor to the soup or stew. Your choice. You can add 1 teaspoon Tarragon to this soup.

** I really like using the Immersion Blender. It is so easy. You don't make such a mess as you do with a blender.

# Mushroom Soup

4 Tablespoons butter
1 ½ pounds white mushrooms, coarsely chopped
2 Portobello mushrooms, stems discarded, chopped
2-3 garlic cloves minced
Salt and pepper to taste
6 cups vegetable broth or water*
¾ cup heavy cream
12 dill sprigs for garnishing
3-4 slices of sourdough bread for garnishing

In a pot, melt butter.
Add mushroom and garlic.
Season with salt and pepper.
Cover and cook over moderate heat for about 5-7 minutes or
    until mushrooms are soft.
Add broth and ½ cup of cream.
Bring to a boil, then simmer, cover for 10-12 minutes.
Puree the soup in food processor or immersion blender.**
Return soup to pot, add salt and pepper to taste and warm.
In a saucepan, bring the remaining ¼ cup of cream to a boil.
Remove from heat and whisk until frothy.
Ladle the soup into a large bowl and top with froth cream
  and garnish with the dill.
Garnish with a slice of mushroom. Crusty bread.
Serves 5-6

# Mushroom Lover's Soup for two

1 large onion, diced
2 -4 Tablespoons olive oil
10 oz white button mushrooms, sliced
10 oz baby Portobello mushrooms
10 stalks fresh thyme, leaves removed
1 cup vegetable broth
1 Tablespoon flour
1 cup almond or cashew milk—unsweetened
1 dried bay leaf
½ Tablespoon soy sauce
Salt and Pepper to taste

In a large soup pot, add a small amount of oil over medium
    heat, add diced onions.
Cook for 5-7 minutes, then add mushrooms and cook 5 more.
Add fresh thyme and continue to cook for 10 minutes.
Add bay leaf, salt and pepper, and soy sauce.
Add flour and stir. Add milk and cook for 15 minutes. Remove bay leaf.
Add Parmesan cheese as garnish.
Serves 5-6

# Corn Chowder

2 cups corn canned (or off the cob) drained, reserve liquid
3 cups chicken broth or chicken cubes in 3 cups water
½ teaspoon sugar and ½ teaspoon sugar, divided
½ cup onion, minced
¼ cup celery, minced
¼ cup butter
½ teaspoon dry mustard
Salt and pepper to taste
1 Tablespoon lemon juice (fresh is best)
1 ½ cups diced potatoes
3 drops Tabasco
½ teaspoon Worcestershire sauce
Pinch thyme
Parsley to taste
Paprika
1 egg yolk-beaten
1 cup heavy cream (small container)
3 Tablespoons flour
3 Tablespoons milk

Put chicken stock, liquid from corn, ½ teaspoon sugar and
　　salt and pepper, simmer for 10-15 minutes.
Sauté corn, onions and celery in butter adding mustard, ½
　　teaspoon of sugar and salt and pepper.
Put sautéed mix in broth with lemon juice and potatoes.
Allow to reach a slow boil. Cook until potatoes are tender.
Turn down heat and add Tabasco and Worcestershire sauce.
Wire whisk yolk and heavy cream in a bowl, then add ½
　　cup of the hot soup stock to the bowl and wire whisk,
　　then add to the remaining soup.
Make a thickening sauce with the 3 Tablespoons flour and
　　milk and wire whisk into the soup slowly to thicken.
Serves 5-6

This is from my first book, In Addition... to the Entrée.

This was my oldest son's favorite recipe to make when he was young. He would stand on a chair and put this together adding something new each time. You can do that too. Have fun and use your imagination.

My son would add:
½ cup red peppers to the sauté or

Red bliss potatoes instead of regular potatoes.

Oregano

Basil

Use your imagination.

This is great on a cold day and you need something to stick to your ribs.

Garnish with croutons or paprika or parsley.

I serve the chowder with thick crusty bread.

©Connie Hope

There is nothing that tastes better than a warm potato soup. Whether you like it with cheese or chunked potatoes or blend it smooth, it will always warm you and will always taste great.

*I like a white cheese instead of cheddar.

Variations:
Add 1/2 cup celery and ¼ teaspoon red pepper flakes to margarine and onions.
Or
Add 1 teaspoon dill with salt and pepper.
Or
Puree mixture before adding ham. This will make a smooth soup rather than chunky.

# Potato Soup

3 large red potatoes, peeled and cubed
2 ½ cups water
1 small onion, finely chopped
3 Tablespoons butter or margarine
3 Tablespoons flour
Salt and fresh pepper to taste
2 ½ cups milk
Pinch of sugar
1 cup ham, cubed
1 cup shredded cheddar cheese (optional)*

Put 2 ½ cups water in pot, add potatoes and cook until
  tender.
Drain potatoes and reserve liquid. Make sure liquid
  measures at least 1 cup. Set both aside.
In a large pot, melt butter or margarine and add onion.
Stir and cook until tender.
Add flour to soup pot, salt and pepper, cook 4 minutes.
This will thicken the liquid.
Add potatoes, reserved liquid, milk and sugar to onions in soup pot.
Add the ham and the cheese, which is optional.
Simmer over low heat for 30-40 minutes.
Serve with crusty bread.
Serves 4-6

Potato Soup © Connie Hope

# Tomato Soup

2 Tablespoons olive oil
1 Tablespoon butter
1 onion, finely chopped
1-2 cloves garlic, minced
2 Tablespoons flour
3 cups chicken broth (or use Clamato or Tomato Juice)
1 (28 oz) can plum tomatoes, pureed
1 teaspoon thyme
Salt and pepper to taste
3 Tablespoons either fresh basil, chives, or dill*
Croutons for garnishing

Use an immersion blender and puree the plum tomatoes.
In a soup pot, heat the oil and butter add the onions, and
  garlic, cook and stir occasionally about 8 minutes.
Add flour and stir to coat the onions and garlic.
Add the broth, tomatoes, thyme, salt and pepper.
Bring to a simmer and stir occasionally for 40-50 minutes
Let cool and puree with a food processor or an immersion blender.
Return to pot and reheat.
Garnish with croutons.

# Jersey Fresh Tomato Soup

7 cups tomato, peeled, seeded, and chopped
1 cup carrots, finely chopped
1 large onion, chopped
1 (13.75oz) can chicken broth
Salt and pepper to taste
3 Tablespoons flour
1 cup milk
2 teaspoons basil, dried
½ teaspoon celery salt
¼ teaspoon garlic powder

Cook tomatoes, carrots and onion on medium heat.
Then reduce add the chicken broth and simmer for 30-40 minutes.
  Stir, adding the salt and pepper.
Melt butter in a sauce pan and whisk in the flour until thick.
Slowly whisk in the milk until smooth, heat for 5 minutes.
Stir milk mixture into the soup pot.
Add basil, celery salt, and garlic powder.
Simmer on low for about 40-50 minutes or until thickens.
You can use an immersion blender and puree the mixture.
Or you can leave it a little chunky.

* Or you can use 1 Tablespoon each.

I am from New Jersey, so this soup recipe grew up with me.

You can use any type of tomato, but Jersey Tomatoes are the best!

# Tomato and Fennel Soup

2 Tablespoons olive oil
1 clove garlic, minced
1 ½ cups  chopped fennel (about one small fennel bulb)
1 medium yellow onion, chopped fine
2 cans  (28 oz) diced tomatoes, drained and reserve the
    liquid
1 Tablespoon fresh rosemary, chopped
1 teaspoon fresh thyme, chopped
$^1/_8$ teaspoon basil
½ teaspoon red pepper flakes
2 cups chicken broth (or vegetable broth or water)
1 teaspoon sugar
Salt and pepper to taste
¼ cup fresh parsley, chopped
½ cup heavy cream

In a soup pot add oil, fennel, onions and garlic and
    cook until translucent. (about 3-5 minutes)
Add the tomatoes, rosemary, pepper flakes, thyme and
    cook for 5-10 minutes.
Add reserved tomato liquid, chicken broth, sugar, and salt
    and pepper to taste.
Reduce to low heat and simmer covered  until fennel is very
    tender (45 minutes to one hour).
Add parsley and puree mixture until smooth.
Return to soup pot and reheat, mix in cream and serve.
Serves 4-6


# Curried Tomato Soup

2 medium onions, chopped
1-2 cloves garlic, finely chopped
2 Tablespoons butter or margarine
1 ½ teaspoons curry powder
2 cans diced tomatoes, chunky
3 cups chicken broth
1 bay leaf
Salt and pepper to taste
Yogurt or ranch dressing for garnish

Saute onion and garlic in butter until tender 3-4 minutes.
Stir in curry, heat for another 3 minutes.
Add tomatoes, chicken broth, bay leaf, salt and pepper.
Bring to boil, then simmer 10 minutes. Remove bay leaf.
Puree soup using an immersion blender or a food processor.
Serve with a dollop of yogurt or ranch dressing.

# Tomato Basil Soup

¼ cup olive oil (or less)
2 carrots, peeled and chopped
½ large yellow onion, chopped
1-2 cloves of garlic, minced*
2 Tablespoons dried basil
2 cans (14.5 oz or 1 can 29 oz) tomato puree
1 can (14.5 oz) diced tomatoes
3 cups chicken broth **
Salt and pepper to taste
1/4 cup fresh basil cut for garnish

Warm oil and add carrots, onion and dried basil.
Saute until tender.
Add cans of tomato puree mix. Bring to a boil.
Reduce and simmer for 10 minutes so flavor blends.
Puree soup in food processor.
Return to pot and heat.
Add salt and pepper to taste. Garnish with basil.
Serves 5-6

© Connie Hope Tomato Basil Soup

# Creamy Tomato Basil Soup

4 tomatoes, peeled, seeded and diced (or use whole tomato
    in a can 29 oz)
4 cups tomato juice
14 leaves fresh basil
1 Tablespoon dried basil
1 cup heavy whipping cream. *
¼ cup butter
Salt and pepper to taste

Simmer tomatoes, juice, basil in pot for at least 30 minutes.
Puree tomato mixture.
Put puree mixture in pot and heat on medium.
Stir in cream and butter (or variation)
Heat until melted. Do Not Boil.
Serves 5-6

Tomato soup is one of my favorites. It is my true comfort food. That and a grilled cheese sandwich. Yum. It's making me hungry.

 * To kick up the flavor and heat just a little, I add 1 teaspoon jarred jalapeno sliced peppers and add when you puree mix. Depends on how spicy you like your food.

 **I have substituted Clamato or Beefomato ® instead of plain tomato juice. Or half and half with the chicken broth and tomato juice. Just adds a little different taste

Variation:
Take out the heavy whipping cream
    and substitute 1 cup milk and 4 oz of
    cream cheese.
Stir in butter and milk and wire whisk
    the cream cheese into the mix until
    melted and blended smoothly.

©Connie Hope Cream Tomato Basil Soup

If you want to add a piece of ham to this or use chicken broth instead of the vegetable broth, you can. It would make it just White Bean Soup

* If you prefer a soup that is smoother, take about half of the soup mixture and puree it in the food processor or immersion blender, then put the puree mixture back into the soup pot and reheat.

*If you want to make this vegan, use soy milk and vegan cheese.

# Vegetarian White Bean Soup

1 cup dried white beans(small navy)
¼ cup butter or margarine
1 large onion, yellow, finely chopped
1 clove garlic, finely chopped
1 large carrot, finely chopped
1 stalk celery, finely chopped
5 cups vegetable broth
1 can plum tomatoes with juice
1 teaspoon dried thyme (or fresh)
1 teaspoon sugar
1 bay leaf
Salt and pepper to taste
1 Tablespoon fresh parsley, finely chopped

Put dried beans in cold water and soak overnight (12 hours).
In a large pot, melt butter and saute onions, carrots, garlic
   and celery for about 3 minutes or until translucent.
Drain beans and add to saute mixture.
Add broth, tomatoes, thyme, bay leaf, sugar, salt & pepper.
Bring to a boil then reduce to low, cover and simmer for 2-
   3 hours. Remove bay leaf.
This will make a chunky soup.*
Garnish with a little parsley and serve in bowls.
Serves 6-8

# Vegetable and Corn Chowder

1 teaspoon olive oil
1 red onion, chopped finely
1 red pepper, seeded and diced finely
3-4 cloves of garlic, minced
1 large potato, peeled and diced
2 Tablespoons flour
2 ½ cups milk*
1 ¼ cups vegetable stock
3 cups corn, drained
1 ½ cups broccoli florets
¾ cup Cheddar cheese, grated
Salt and pepper to taste

Heat the oil, add onion, pepper, garlic, potato for 3 minutes.
Stir in flour, then gradually add milk and vegetable stock.
Add broccoli, corn, bring to a boil then simmer 30 minutes.
Salt and pepper, stir in ½ the cheese, garnish with the rest.
Serves 4-5

# Vegetable Soup

1 medium onion, thinly sliced
1 Tablespoon olive oil
4 cups vegetable broth
1 cup zucchini, chunked, cleaned
1 (15 ½ oz) navy beans, rinsed and drained
½ cup potatoes, peeled and diced*
½ cup green beans, fresh, cut in 1 inch pieces
½ cup tomato, peeled and chopped
Salt and pepper to taste
1/8 teaspoon ground turmeric
2 Tablespoons tomato paste

Saute onion in oil until tender.
Add veggie broth, zucchini, beans, potatoes, green beans
   tomato, salt, pepper, turmeric.
Bring to a boil, reduce, cover, and simmer for 30 minutes.
Stir in tomato paste.
Serves 4-5

# Garden Vegetable Soup

4 Tablespoons olive oil
2 ½ cups leeks, chopped, white part only
2-3 cloves garlic, minced
2 cups carrots, peeled and cut into rounds ½ inch thick
2 cups potatoes, peeled and diced
2 cups fresh green beans, ends cut, cut into 1 inch pieces
8 cups vegetable broth (you can also use chicken)
4 cups tomatoes, peeled, seeded and chopped
2 cups corn (you can use on the cob if you have it)
Salt and pepper to taste
¼ cup fresh parsley leaves, chopped and packed
2-3 teaspoons lemon juice (fresh is best)

Heat oil in pot, add leeks and garlic. Cook 8-10 minutes.
Add carrots, potatoes, green beans and continue to cook 5-6
   minutes, stirring occasionally.
Add broth, bring to a boil, then reduce and simmer.
Add tomatoes, corn, salt and pepper.
Reduce and add parsley and lemon juice.
Serve with crusty bread.
Serves 5-6

* Using red potatoes gives this soup a hearty flavor.

Variation:
add 1 cup celery, chopped
Or
½ teaspoon thyme
Or
1 cup peas
Or
1 cup zucchini

It has 8 cups of vegetables, mix them any way you'd like.

# Garden Vegetable Soup-Variation

¼ pound mushrooms; sliced
4 onions, chopped
2 Tablespoons olive oil
5 carrots cut into1/2 inch pieces
4 stalks celery, cut into ½ inch pieces
1 10 oz frozen package of okra cut into ½ inch pieces
2 medium zucchini, cut into ½ inch pieces
1 can (28 oz) whole tomatoes
1 can (16 oz) whole tomatoes
1 teaspoon basil
Salt and pepper to taste

Saute mushrooms and onions in 2 Tablespoons oil.
Low heat for 2-3 minutes or until soft.
Add remaining ingredients.
Bring to a boil, then lower and simmer for 30-40 minutes.
Serves 4-5.

Garden Vegetable Soup-Variation© Connie Hope

# Creamy Green Pea Soup

3 cups peas, fresh or frozen
2 Tablespoons onion, chopped
2 Tablespoons parsley, chopped
½ cup water
1 tall can of Pet Evaporated Milk (about 1 2/3 cups)
1 Tablespoon chives, chopped
Salt and pepper to taste

Cook peas, onion and parsley in water until tender, 20-25
    minutes in a soup pot.
Pour cooked peas mixture and evaporated milk into blender
    and whir until smooth.  (Can use an immersion blender).
Return mixture to soup pot.
Add chives, salt and pepper and heat until steaming hot.
Makes 4 servings.

# Spinach Soup

2 pounds fresh spinach
8 cups chicken broth
1 clove garlic, chopped
1 small onion, chopped
3 Tablespoons cornmeal
1 Tablespoon flour
Salt and pepper to taste
¼ teaspoon nutmeg

Rinse spinach, remove stems.
In a large pot, combine 1 cup broth, garlic and onion.
Bring to a boil, then add spinach and cook for 2 minutes.
Add remaining broth and bring to a boil.
In a small bowl, combine cornmeal and flour, slowly
    add to broth stirring as you pour.
Cover and simmer for 30 minutes.
Puree soup in food processor, add salt, pepper and nutmeg.
Serves 6-8

# Zucchini-Basil Soup

1 ½ pound zucchini
3 Tablespoons butter
1 onion, chopped
2 cloves garlic
1/3 cup basil leaves, packed
6 cups chicken broth
½ cup rice, uncooked
Salt and pepper to taste
Grated parmesan cheese

Clean and cut ends off zucchini; shred with grater.
In a large pot, melt butter, add onions and cook 2-3 minutes.
Add zucchini and basil and heat, then add stock and rice.
Bring to a boil, then reduce and simmer for 30 minutes.
Puree in blender or immersion blender and return to pot.
Add salt and pepper and return to warm.
Serve with parmesan cheese and basil leaf.
Serves 4-6

This is a soup my mother, Blanche, loved. On a cold winter day, she would put this together for a Saturday treat.
Thanks, mom.

Cooking should always have experimental thinking involved.

You can also use beef broth instead of chicken to change the taste.

You can substitute 1 can of cream of chicken soup or cream of celery soup for 1 cup of broth. It adds an interesting taste.

Additions:
Add 3 potatoes, peeled and diced
Add 2 Tablespoons chopped fresh dill
Or
¼ teaspoon dried thyme or rosemary.

* You can use two sizes of lima beans, small or large.

* You can use the pre-cooked bacon strips and just warm them and crumble.

# Lima Bean Chowder

2 boxes (32 oz) chicken broth
2 cans (15 ¼ oz) lima beans, rinsed and drained*
3 medium carrots, sliced thin
2 potatoes, peeled and diced
2 red peppers, chopped
2 onions, medium, chopped
2-3 stalks of celery, sliced thin
¼ cup butter
1 ½ teaspoons dried marjoram
½ teaspoon dried oregano
Salt and pepper to taste
1 cup half and half cream
3-4 strips of bacon, cooked and crumbled*

In a soup pot add the first eleven ingredients.
Bring to a boil, then reduce heat, and simmer for 30-40
    minutes or until veggies are tender.
Add cream, and heat through, but do not boil.
Before serving, sprinkle with bacon.

# White Bean Chowder

2 Tablespoons olive oil
3 slices bacon, minced
1 onion, finely chopped
1-2 stalks celery, finely chopped
1 carrot, finely diced
½ red bell pepper, finely diced
2-3 cloves of garlic, minced
2 teaspoons fresh thyme, minced leaves
1 ½ teaspoons flour
3 cups vegetable broth ( or chicken)
1 tomato, finely diced
1 Tablespoon tomato paste
1 bay leaf
¼ teaspoon dried oregano
Salt and pepper to taste
1 can (15oz) cannellini beans, rinsed and drained
3 Tablespoons heavy cream.
2 Tablespoons fresh parsley leaves for garnish.

Heat oil to medium, cook bacon, add onion, celery, carrot,
    and bell pepper, cook until soft—5 minutes.
Simmer and add garlic and thyme, slowly stir in flour.
Add broth, tomato, tomato paste, bay leaf, oregano, salt,
    pepper and beans ,bring to a boil, then simmer 20 minutes.
Turn heat off and stir in cream and parsley.
Serves 3-4

# Navy Bean Soup

3 cans ( 16 oz ) navy beans, rinsed and drained
1 can (14 ½ oz) diced tomatoes, undrained
1 large onion, chopped
1 ham bone or 1 cup diced cooked ham
2 cups chicken broth*
2 ½ cup water
Salt and pepper to taste
1 teaspoon dried thyme
½ teaspoon marjoram
½ teaspoon sage
Parsley for garnishing

Place beans in a soup kettle and add broth and water.
Add the tomatoes, onion, ham bone or ham pieces, salt and
    pepper and spices.
Bring to a boil, then reduce heat and simmer for 1 ½ hours.
Remove ham bone and let cook.
Cut bite-size pieces off ham bone and put in the soup.
If you want a thicker soup, take out 1-2 cups of soup and
    puree it with an immerse blender, then return to soup.
Heat and serve with parsley.
Serves 6-8

Navy Bean Soup © Connie Hope

*I use 'Better than Bouillon' in the ham broth.

You can also use it in the 2 ½ cups of water.

# White Bean Fennel Soup

1 large onion, chopped
1 small bulb of fennel, sliced thin
1 Tablespoon olive oil
5 cups chicken broth (can use vegetable broth)
1 (15 oz) can white kidney beans or cannellini beans rinsed
    and drained.
1 (14 ½ oz) diced tomatoes, not drained
1 teaspoon thyme
Salt and pepper to taste
1 bay leaf
3 cups fresh spinach (I prefer baby spinach) stems trimmed

In a soup pot, saute onion and fennel in oil until tender.
Add broth, beans, tomatoes, spices and bring to a boil.
Reduce heat, cover and simmer for 30-40 minutes.
Fennel should be tender. Discard bay leaf, add spinach.
Cook 4-5 minutes until spinach is wilted.
Serves 4-5

# The French Onion Soup 101

Onion soup can be credited to ancient Greek and Rome. The onion soup was called the poor people's food because it is cheap and easy to grow.

It is said that the first French onion soup was invented by King Louis XV of France. He wanted a late evening snack. There was nothing in the hunting lodge except butter, onions and champagne. According to the tale, he combined these three ingredients to create the first French Onion Soup. Not sure how true this tale is, but it makes a nice story!*

French onion soup is one of the most popular soup recipes in homes and restaurants. It is also a very simple and easy soup to prepare. There are many different recipes for French Onion Soup. These are several of mine. They are quick and easy and really taste great. Traditional French onion soups is a combination of rich beef broth and sweet, caramelized onions, topped with bread (French bread) and melted cheese. It is a great combination of wonderful flavors. You taste the sweetness from the caramelized onions and the sharpness of the cheese with the rich flavor of the beef broth.

Many different kinds of cheese can be used. The classic French onion soup uses Gruyere cheese. Gruyere has a sweet and a slightly salty taste, and is a hard yellow cheese from Switzerland. Some not as traditional French onion soups use cheddar, mozzarella, Parmesan and provolone cheese. Wow, it's making me hungry just writing about this soup.

You can even make a vegan or vegetarian version of this soup. A vegetarian or vegan version soup uses vegetable broth instead of beef broth and uses Vegan (non dairy) cheese.

"The Process of making a good onion soup is somewhat like the process of learning to love.
It requires commitment,
extraordinary effort, time and it may make you cry"
Ronnie Lundy

*Wikipedia

Sweet Yellow Onion French Onion Soup © Connie Hope

# Simple French Onion Soup

3 Tablespoons butter
6 Vidalia onions, sliced thin (or sweet onions)
2-3 garlic cloves, minced
1 Tablespoon sugar
3 cans beef broth (15 oz) or box of 48 oz
1 beef cube (1 use 1 teaspoon Bovril)*
Salt and pepper to taste
1 teaspoon dried thyme
1 bay leaf
2 Tablespoons dry sherry—optional (or white wine)
3 slices French Bread toasted **(1 inch thick)
3 slices Provolone cheese***
3 Tablespoons grated Parmesan cheese

Melt butter and saute onions very slowly until they are
    golden brown, about 40-50 minutes.
Add garlic and sugar about 30 minutes into cooking the onions.
Add beef broth and beef cube (or Bovril) and sherry or wine.
Simmer 20-30 minutes.
Place into an oven crock.
Put bread slices and cheese on each crock.
Broil for 5 minutes or until cheese is melted.
Or you can put in microwave for 30 seconds to melt
    the cheese. The toast may get a little soft.
Serve immediately.
Serves 3.

*What the heck is Bovril? It is a British Beef Extract. It has a very thick beefy/salty taste. I use it in soups, stews, and just as a broth by itself. It is really tasty and adds lots of flavor to whatever you are cooking. "The Original Beef Extract"

Options:
1 teaspoon paprika
1 bay leaf
Add with beef broth and beef cubes.

Remove the dry sherry and use a half cup brandy.

You can also use chicken broth instead of beef or, if you want it vegetarian, use vegetable broth.

**Here are two methods to toast French bread.
1. Put in toaster or toaster oven and heat until lightly brown.
2. Heat oven to 325 degrees. Put slices on a cookie tray and heat until browned.

***Or use shredded Gruyere cheese (2 Tablespoons on each Crock. I prefer this.). It can be substituted for the Provolone cheese, Swiss cheese or another of your favorite cheeses.

French Onion Soup with Gruyere Cheese © Connie Hope

*How to caramelize Onions  see next page

*You can use chicken broth, or a combination of the two.

Traditionally, French Onion soup is made with beef broth.

** This aids in the carmelization of the onions.

# French Onion Soup—Variation # 1

3-4 Tablespoons butter or margarine
2 large red onions, thinly sliced
2 large yellow onions, thinly sliced
64 oz beef broth
½ cup red wine (or use a dry sherry if you prefer)
I Tablespoon Worcestershire sauce
2-3 sprigs fresh parsley
I sprig fresh thyme
I bay leaf
I Tablespoon balsamic vinegar
Salt and pepper to taste
4 slices French bread (cut one inch thick)
8 slices of Swiss or Gruyere cheese

Melt margarine in large soup pot.
Stir in salt and pepper, red onion, and sweet onions.
Cook for 30-40 minutes, very slowly.
Stirring frequently until onions start to caramelize*
Add beef broth, red wine and Worcestershire sauce.
Bundle herbs with kitchen twine and place in pot.
Simmer for 20-30 minutes, stirring frequently.
Remove herbs and mix in vinegar.
Prepare bread and bake with cheese. (see methods to toast bread and bake cheese 'The French Onion Soup 101').
Serves 4-5

# French Onion Soup-Variation # 2

6 large yellow onions(try red onions) peeled and thinly sliced
3-5 Tablespoons of Olive oil
¼ teaspoon sugar
2-3 cloves garlic, minced
8 cups of beef broth*
½ cup dry vermouth or dry white wine
I bay leaf
¼ teaspoon thyme, dried
Salt and pepper to taste
8 slices of French bread, toasted
I ½ cups Swiss Gruyere Cheese, grated

In a large pot, saute the onions in the olive oil on medium to
    low heat until well browned, 30-40 plus minutes.
Add sugar about 10 minutes into cooking the onions. **
Add garlic and continue to saute for several minutes.
Add the stock, vermouth or wine, bay leaf, and thyme.
Cover and simmer for 30 minutes. Salt and pepper.
Serve in oven proof bowls, add toast and cheese and broil
    for a few minutes,
Serves 4-6

# The Onion Soup—The French Onion Soup
## Vegetarian or Vegan

You can even make a vegan or vegetarian version of this soup. A vegetarian or vegan onion soup uses vegetable broth instead of beef broth and uses Vegan (non dairy) cheese. You can top with French bread as well.

## French Onion Soup(Vegan)

2 Tablespoons vegan butter
4 large sweet onions, sliced
1 teaspoon sugar
Salt and pepper to taste
1 bay leaf
1 teaspoon dried thyme or 1 Tablespoon fresh thyme
1 teaspoon Dijon mustard
3 Tablespoon soy sauce
¼ cup red wine
6 cup vegetable broth

Heat butter in large pot. Add onions, sugar and cook slowly
    for 45 minutes to 1 hours or until onions are
    caramelized.*
Stir frequently.
Add the bay leaf, thyme, wine, soy sauce, mustard, salt and
    pepper. Stir.
Add vegetable broth and bring to a quick boil; then lower
    heat and simmer for 30 minutes.
Serve with croutons or crusty bread.
Serves 4-6

Vegetarian French Onion Soup © Connie Hope

*How to caramelize onions:

Slowly cook the onions with a little olive oil until they are a rich brown color. Onions are naturally sweet and the caramelizing comes when the onions are cooked slowly over extended periods of time and their natural sugars are released.

This recipe is from In Addition... to the Entrée, my first cookbook.

Perhaps this doesn't sound good, but it is a great soup for warm weather or anytime. I went to a luncheon with my two long time friends and Bev served this. It was delicious! Thanks , Bev

# Honey Dew Soup (Cold)

1 cucumber (If you use 1 hot house, it has no seeds If you use 2 regular cucumbers, scoop the seeds out with a teaspoon.)
2 cups honey dew melon
8 oz plain non fat yogurt
¼ cup fresh mint, cleaned
2 ½ Tablespoons fresh lime juice
Salt and pepper to taste
Mint leaf for decoration and a wedge of lime

Whirl all ingredients in a food processor or blender.
Chill for several hours. Serves 4-6
Garnish with fresh mint and serve with a wedge of lime.

Honey Dew Soup © Connie Hope

# Corn Chowder-Vegan

2 Tablespoons olive oil
1 cup onions, chopped
6 cups corn ( use frozen, or canned)
3 cups vegetable broth
½ cup red bell pepper, chopped
½ teaspoon fresh rosemary, chopped
½ teaspoon dried thyme
¼ teaspoon cayenne
Salt and pepper to taste

Put oil in a large soup pot.
Saute onion for 5-8 minutes or until translucent.
Add 4 cups corn, 2 cups broth, simmer 20-30 minutes.
Remove from heat.
Use an immersion blender and puree until smooth.
Return to heat
Add bell pepper, rosemary and thyme.
Salt and pepper to taste, cayenne, remaining corn and broth.
Simmer for 15-20 minutes.
Garnish with a few pieces of rosemary.
Serves 4

# Lima Bean Soup

1-2 Tablespoons olive oil
1-2 cloves of garlic
3 cups cooked lima beans (frozen or canned)
2 cups chicken broth
1 onion, diced
Fresh herbs, chopped ( you can use thyme, rosemary,
    marjoram, basil or anything you choose)
Salt and pepper to taste
2 sausage, sliced and cooked  (optional)

In a large pot, add oil and garlic then lima beans.
Cook 3-4 minutes, then add the chicken broth.
Cook until beans are tender about 5 minutes.
Add seasonings, and heat for 5 minutes.
Put bean mix in the food processor and puree until smooth.
Put in pot. Add sausages, reheat. Serve hot with crusty breads.
Serves 2-3

My children will never forgive me
for this soup.  They really dislike
lima beans.  I tried making this soup
thinking they would try it.  Wrong!
Anyway, my girlfriend and I really
liked the taste and eat it often.

# Lentil Soup

1 Tablespoon olive oil
4 cloves of garlic, finely chopped
2 carrots, finely chopped
2 stalks celery, chopped
1 yellow onion, chopped
1 cup dried lentils
1 (14 oz) can diced tomatoes with liquid
1 cup finely chopped ham
1 ham bone (optional)
6 sprigs thyme, fresh
1 teaspoon dried thyme
1 teaspoon dried rosemary
½ teaspoon dried sage
½ teaspoon dried tarragon
1 bay leaf
8 cups chicken broth, divided
Salt and pepper to taste

Heat oil, add garlic, carrots, celery, and onions. Cook until
    soft. 5-7 minutes.
Stir in lentils, tomatoes, ham, ham bone, and spices.
Add 4 cups broth, cover and simmer for 30 minutes. Stir.
Add more broth and cook 45 minutes longer. Remove bay
    leaf and ham bone.
Serves 4-6

# Lentil Spinach Soup

½ pound Italians turkey sausage
1 small onion, chopped
4 cups water
½ cup dried lentils, rinsed
2 teaspoons chicken bouillon
1/8 teaspoon red pepper flakes
1 package (10 oz) fresh spinach, chopped
2 Tablespoon shredded Parmesan cheese

In a large soup pot, cook sausage and onion until no longer
     pink.
Stir in water, lentils, bouillon, and red pepper flakes.
Bring to a boil.
Reduce heat, cover and simmer for 30-40 minutes or until
     lentils are tender.
Stir in spinach, cook 5-7 minutes longer.  Spinach should be
     tender.
Sprinkle with cheese.
Serves 4

* your choice

** Optional: If you have a ham hock,
you can put that in the pot when
you are simmering for 1 hour, then
remove it.

# Lentil Soup

1 Tablespoon olive oil
1 ½ cups onions, diced
1 cup carrots, diced
½ cup celery, diced
1 clove garlic
1 bay leaf
2 teaspoons fresh herbs or 1 teaspoon dried herbs *
1 cup rinsed lentils
6 cups chicken broth
½ lemon, juiced
Salt and pepper to taste
2 scallions, sliced thin for garnishing

In a large pot, add oil and heat onions for about 8 minutes
     until tender.
Add carrots, celery, garlic, bay leaf, and herbs and saute for
     10 minutes on low.
Add lentils, and chicken broth and bring to a boil; then
     lower heat, cover, and simmer for 1 hour. **
Stir in lemon juice, salt and pepper.
Serve hot and garnish with scallions.
Serves 4-6

# Lentil Soup with Sausage

½ pound lentils
4 cups Vegetable broth (or you can use chicken broth)
½ cup carrots, diced
½ cup onions, minced
1-2 cloves of garlic, minced
½ cup celery, chopped
2 Tablespoons butter
Salt and pepper to taste
1 bay leaf
½ teaspoon thyme
1-2 Tablespoons flour
2 cups sliced sausage
Dry sherry
Sour cream as garnish

Combine lentils, broth, vegetables and all spices.
Cover, boil, then simmer 1 ½ hours or until lentils are tender.
Remove bay leaf.
Melt butter in measuring cup, then sprinkle flour. Mix well.
Gradually add to soup and stir until slightly thickened.
If you want a thinner soup, add a little more broth.
Serve with ½ Tablespoon of dry sherry, and sour cream.
Serves 4-6

# Pasta Bean Soup

1 onion, chopped
1 large carrot, chopped
1-2 stalks celery, chopped
2 Tablespoons olive oil
2-3 cloves of garlic, minced
4 cups chicken broth (or vegetable)
¾ cup uncooked small pasta
1 ½ teaspoons Italian seasoning
¼ teaspoon red pepper flakes
2 (15 oz) cans white kidney or cannellini beans, rinsed,
    drained
1 (28 oz) can crushed tomatoes
3 Tablespoons Parmesan cheese, grated

In soup pot, saute onion, carrot, and celery in oil until tender.
Add garlic, saute. Add the broth, pasta, Italian seasoning and
    pepper flakes.
Bring to a boil, reduce and simmer for 15-20 minutes until
    pasta is tender.
Add beans and tomatoes, simmer for 15 minutes. Garnish
    with Parmesan cheese.
Serves 5-6

Variations:

1 can (14 ½ oz) tomatoes diced
3 Tablespoons Dijon mustard

# Split Pea Soup

1 pound green split peas (in a bag)
2 Tablespoons oil
10 cups of chicken broth or other vegetable broth*
1 onion, chopped
3 carrots diced
1 cup celery, chopped
Bay leaf
Parsley
Salt and pepper to taste
Ham bone if you have it
3-4 pieces of ham, chopped

Wash and drain peas.
Add oil in a large soup pot and sauté onions, carrots, celery.
Simmer for 5 minutes until onions are transparent.
Add the remaining ingredients and bring to a boil.
Lower heat to simmer, slowly, for 2 hours.
If you like a smooth puree pea soup, put in the food
    processor or immersion blender, or just leave it as is with
    the vegetables and peas chunky.
Serves 6-8.
Serve with croutons.

Pureed Pea Soup© Connie Hope

Pea Soup not pureed © Connie Hope

# Broccoli Soup

1 ½ cup chicken broth
½ cup chopped onion
2 cups chopped broccoli
½ teaspoon salt
2 dashes white pepper
½ teaspoon dried thyme
1 bay leaf
Dash garlic powder
1 cup milk
2 Tablespoons butter
2 Tablespoons flour

Combine chicken broth, onions, and spices with broccoli.
Bring to boil, reduce heat, simmer for 10 minutes.
Remove bay leaf. Puree with immersion blender.
Put mixture back into soup pot.
Melt butter, add flour and milk to make a white sauce.
Add white sauce to the broccoli mixture in the pot.
Heat for another 20 minutes, until thicken.
Serves 4-6

# Cream of Broccoli Soup

2 pounds broccoli
½ cup onions, chopped
¼ green pepper, minced
2 Tablespoons butter
2 Tablespoons flour
6 cups chicken stock (or use vegetable stock)
1 bay leaf
3-4 parsley sprigs
1 teaspoon thyme
¼ teaspoon nutmeg
Salt and pepper to taste
2-3 egg yolks
1 cup heavy cream

Saute broccoli, onions, peppers in butter until brown.
Sprinkle in the flour and stir for 2-3 minutes.
Add stock and tie the bay leaf, parsley and thyme together.
Stir until smooth. Bring to a boil, simmer for 30-40 minutes.
Remove tied spices. Puree in blender or immersion blender.
Add nutmeg, salt, pepper. Beat egg yolks & cream in bowl.
Whisk ½ cup of hot soup, then return to soup pot.
Serves 6

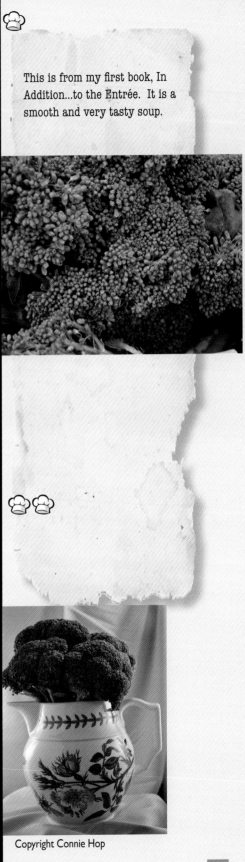

This is from my first book, In Addition...to the Entrée. It is a smooth and very tasty soup.

Copyright Connie Hop

Variations:

½ teaspoon cumin
½ teaspoon basil

Can double the amount of Velveeta cheese if you like it really cheesy.

Instead of Velveeta cheese, you can use sharp cheddar.

Can add some cauliflower florets.

Can also add a cup of chopped ham for a richer taste.

*White sauce:
2 Tablespoons butter
2-3 Tablespoons Flour
1 cup milk or half and half
Melt butter and slowly mix in flour to make a paste.
Slowly add milk to flour mixture, stirring with a wire whisk continually over warm heat. Always stir in the same direction. Mixture will thicken

# Broccoli and Cheese Soup

Cooking spray
1 cup onions, chopped
2-3 cloves of garlic, minced
3 cups chicken broth(can substitute vegetable broth)
1 (16 ox) package broccoli florets
2 ½ cups milk
1/3 cup flour
Salt and pepper to taste
8 oz Velveeta cheese, cubed

Spray soup pot with cooking spray over medium heat.
Add onions and garlic and saute for 3-4 minutes.
Add broth and broccoli.
Bring to a boil and then reduce to simmer.
Stir and cook for 10-15 minutes.
Combine the milk and flour and whisk until blended.
Add milk mixture, cook 5-8 minutes or until slightly thick.
Stir in salt and pepper.
Remove from heat and add cheese, stirring until melts.
Either put part in blender and process or use an immersion blender and pureed mixture.
Serves 6

# Broccoli Soup

1 ½ cups chicken broth
½ cup onions, yellow, chopped
Salt and pepper to taste
2 cups chopped broccoli
½ teaspoon dried thyme
1 bay leaf
Dash of garlic powder

Bring chicken broth, chopped onions, broccoli and spices to a boil, then reduce , simmer for 10 minutes.
Remove bay leaf and puree soup in food processor.
Make a white sauce *
Slowly wire whisk into soup mixture until you have the soup to the consistency that you desire.
Heat slowly for another 15 minutes, stirring.
Serves 2-3

# Butternut Squash Soup

8 cups chicken broth (or use vegetable broth)
3 carrots, peeled and sliced thin
5-6 slices bacon, chopped
1 clove garlic, minced
2-3 stalks celery, chopped
2-3 teaspoons chopped parsley
½ teaspoon dried thyme
1 bay leaf
1 large potato, peeled and cubed
1 butternut squash, peeled, seeded and cubed
1 Tablespoon sugar
Salt and pepper to taste
3-5 Tablespoons dark rum*
2 Tablespoons fresh lime juice
Parsley chopped for garnishing

Put broth in a large soup pot over medium heat.
Add carrots, bacon, garlic, celery, parsley, thyme, bay leaf.
Bring to boil, cover and simmer 1 hour over medium heat.
Add potato, squash, sugar and salt and pepper to taste.
Cook 40-50 minutes or until vegetables are tender.
Let cook, remove bay leaf and bacon.
Put into a food processor or immerse blender and puree.
Stir in rum, lime juice, salt, pepper, simmer 7 minutes.
Garnish with parsley.
Serves 7-8

# Golden Squash Soup

3 leeks, just the white part, sliced thin
3-4 medium carrots, chopped
5 Tablespoons butter
3 pounds of butternut squash, peeled and cubed
6 cups chicken broth (can substitute vegetable broth)
3 medium zucchini, peeled and sliced
Salt and pepper to taste
½ teaspoon thyme
1 cup half and half cream
½ cup milk
Cheese or chives for garnishes

Saute leeks and carrots in butter for 5 minutes.
Add squash, broth, zucchini, salt, pepper, thyme.
Bring to a boil, reduce and simmer for 35 -40 minutes.
In a blender or immersion blender, puree soup.
Return to pot and stir in cream and milk, heat.
Sprinkle with cheese and chives.
Serve 5-6.

The butternut squash soup found in In Addition...to the Entrée, my first cookbook, has cream in it. It is equally as good.

* Substitute dry wine for the rum.

You can also use some of the seeds from the squash as a garnish. Makes it look great.

Variations:
• Add 2 cinnamon sticks. Add with potatoes.
Or
• Add 2 Tablespoons brown sugar
Or
• Add 1 Tablespoon fresh ginger root, minced.

# Cabbage Soup

4 ½ cups water
1 ½ cups tomato puree
3 packets or cubes of beef bouillon
2 teaspoons lemon juice
3 cups shredded cabbage
3 medium apples, cored and diced
1/3 cup onion flakes
1 Tablespoon caraway seeds
Artificial sweetener to equal 2 teaspoons sugar
Salt and pepper to taste

Combine water, tomato puree, bouillon and lemon juice in a saucepan.
Stir well and bring to a boil.
Add the remaining ingredients.
Cover and simmer for 20 minutes.
Makes 6 servings

This cabbage is from my garden.
It was huge.

# Red Cabbage Soup

2 pounds of red cabbage, chopped in ¼, then again
1 potato, peeled and cubed
3 cloves of garlic, minced
1 medium onion, chopped
4 cups vegetable or chicken broth
2 Tablespoons blue cheese
2 Tablespoons butter
Salt and pepper to taste

Put butter in a soup pot to melt, then add garlic and onion.
Cook until onion has softened, 5-7 minutes.
Add red cabbage and potato to onion in the soup pot.
Stir vegetables and salt and pepper to taste.
Put lid on pan and cook for 5-6 minutes, stir occasionally.
Add broth, stir. Bring to boil, then simmer 15 minutes.
Remove half of the red cabbage to another bowl.
Cook remaining red cabbage for 5 minutes.
Then blend with immersion blender until smooth.
Put remaining red cabbage in the pot and stir.
Serves 4

Variations:
Add 1 teaspoon Cumin
Add 1 teaspoon Basil

# German Cabbage Soup

1 ½ cups shredded cabbage
2 Tablespoons chopped onion
¼ teaspoon caraway seed
2 Tablespoons butter
1 can cream of potato soup
Salt and pepper to taste
1 can milk

In soup pot, add butter and cook cabbage, onion and
  caraway seeds until tender.
Add cream of potato soup and salt and pepper.
Pour into blender or food processor, blend until smooth.
Or you can leave it chunky.
Return to pot and gradually add milk,
Heat until warm.
Serves 3-4
This is chunky.

German Cabbage Soup © Connie Hope

# Green Soup

1 package (9 oz) frozen creamed spinach, thawed
1 ¼ cups chicken broth*
1/8 teaspoon mace or nutmeg
Salt and pepper to taste
1 medium carrot, coarsely shredded
Minced green onions for garnish

In a sauce pan, heat spinach, broth, nutmeg and salt and
  pepper until hot.
Add the carrots and stir for 5 minutes or until warm.
Garnish with green onions.
Serves 2

I was looking through my mother's
recipe folder and found this. I
remember her making this on a cold
winter day. Yum.

Thanks, Mom.

This one is smooth.

Again, thanks Mom.

* You can substitute cream of celery
soup or cream of spinach soup for
the chicken broth. Then add a half
can each of water and milk.

This recipe was given to me by Aunt Jane. Thanks.

**Hubbard squash** is another cultivar of butternut squash and is usually a 'tear-drop' shape. It is often used as a replacement for pumpkin.

This recipe was in my first cookbook, In Addition...to the Entrée.

Hubbard Squash © Connie Hope

# Hubbard Squash Soup (Butternut Squash Soup)

1 Tablespoon virgin olive oil
1 medium onion, diced fine
½ cup chopped scallions
2 garlic cloves, diced fine
1 quart vegetable broth, chicken broth or water
4 cups Hubbard squash or butternut squash, cubed and cooked (2-3 squash)
1 teaspoon cinnamon
1/4 teaspoon mace
Salt and pepper to taste
1 cup heavy cream (or soy milk thickened with flour and water) The cream is optional. I like it just as well without.

Heat olive oil, sauté the onion, scallions, garlic until golden.

Add the broth and simmer 15-20 minutes.

Add the squash, salt, cinnamon, pepper, and mace.

Simmer for 15 more minutes.

Put in food processor or immersion blender and puree.

Add the heavy cream (or soy, optional).

Continue to simmer until heated throughout.

Garnish with chopped scallion, a dollop of sour cream or pesto (see index) or use your imagination.

Serves 6-8

Hubbard Squash Soup © Connie Hope

## Three Sister's Soup and History

History of the Three Sisters:

The Three Sisters are corn, beans and squash. Native Americans had these 3 main crops. They grew these crops in a companion planting or grouping in the same mounds. The corn provided the ladder for the climbing bean vines. The beans provided the nitrogen to the soil, and the squash covered the ground and prevented weeds. The corn and beans grew together to provided shade for the squash. The three crops benefit each other. Many Native American tribes have other versions of the Three Sisters, but all show the three sisters helped each other and lived harmoniously in the same place.

## Three Sister's Soup

2 cups (19 oz can) corn kernels or use frozen corn
2 cups green beans, chopped in ½ inch pieces
2 cups cubed butternut squash
1 ½ -2 cups potatoes, diced
5 cups vegetable or chicken broth
2 Tablespoons butter or margarine softened
2 Tablespoons flour
Salt and pepper to taste
Herbs of your choice

In a soup pot, combine corn, beans, squash, potatoes, herbs
    and broth.
Bring to a boil, reduce heat, cover, simmer for 1 ½ hours.
This makes a chunky soup. If you prefer smoother, puree in
    food processor.
In a small bowl, blend flour, and butter together and wire
    whisk into soup slowly, stirring continually.
Add salt and pepper to taste. Heat for another 10-15
    minutes on slow simmer.
Serves 6-8

To make any soup Vegan, re-move the beef or chicken broth and use vegetable broth.

You can add many different herbs to change the flavor.

1 teaspoon basil
Or
1 teaspoon thyme
Or
1 teaspoon marjoram
Or
1 teaspoon rosemary

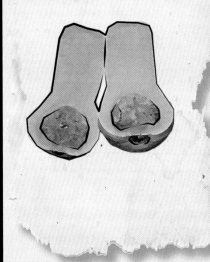

# Kale-Potato Soup with Bacon

3 slices bacon, chopped
1 ¾ pound potatoes, peeled and diced
1 leek (white and green parts only)thin sliced
2 cloves garlic, minced
1 teaspoon chopped fresh rosemary and thyme
Salt and pepper to taste
4 cups chicken broth
2 cups water
1 medium bunch kale, stems removed, leaves chopped
   (about 10 cups)
¾ teaspoon Worcestershire sauce
1 Tablespoon extra-virgin olive oil
1 Tablespoon sour cream
2 Tablespoons chopped, smoked almonds

Cook bacon in large Dutch oven over medium heat, stir
   occasionally until crisp, about 5 minutes.
Remove and drain on paper towel.
Add the potatoes and leeks to drippings in pot and cook,
   stirring about 3 minutes.
Add garlic, herbs, salt and pepper.
Cook until vegetables are slightly browned about 2 minutes.
Add chicken broth and 2 cups of water.
Bring to a boil, cover and cook 15 minutes.
Add 3/4 quarters of the kale, cooking covered until wilted
   about 5 minutes. Stir in Worcestershire sauce.
Preheat the broiler.
Toss the remaining kale with olive oil on a baking sheet, salt
   and pepper and broil until crisp, about 3 minutes.
Thin the sour cream with a splash of water.
Puree the soup in a blender until smooth.
Reheat if needed.
Top with sour cream, kale chips, bacon and almonds.
Serves 4

Kale-Potato Soup with Bacon © Connie Hope

## Connie's Cooking Tips

• Bring your bags to the supermarket. Plastic bags are hard on the environment. Most supermarkets and stores will sell you their store bags; sometimes local seamstresses sell these bags at church bazaars or small stores. They can be reused many, many times and help save our environment.

• Buy meats from certified Human Farm Animal Care vendors. This program is helping to improve the lives of million of farm animals. Check out their website at http://www.certifiedhumane.org/ The program standards includes nutritious diet without antibiotics or hormones, animals raised with shelter, resting areas, sufficient space, and the ability to engage in natural behaviors.

• Grow some of your own veggies and herbs. I have a large container with many herbs for my cooking. I have dill, parsley, rosemary, basil, cilantro, thyme, mint, oregano, sage and chive.

• Collect rain water for your garden and house plants. This helps to save water. Rain water is great for all plants.

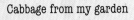
Cabbage from my garden

Herbs in my garden © Connie Hope

# Cold Soups

I was brought up with the idea that a soup should be piping hot and warming on a cold winter day for lunch or dinner as great comfort food. All winter we make rich, thick and hot soups. As the summer heats up (and in Florida it does heat up), it is nice to cool down with a cold soup (a.k.a. summer soup or chilled soups all good alternative words.) I have really been won over to using these cold (chilled) soups. Now, don't get me wrong, I still make plenty of hot soups also in the summer. But making of cold soups is fun and a taste treat. And I love to have fun making things that taste great in my kitchen.

While the two most popular cold soups we know are the tomato based Spanish Gazpacho which combines onions, peppers, and tomato, and the vichyssoise made with leeks, potatoes, wine, and cream. In today's culinary world there are many, many more delicious and creative cold soups. Cold soups are usually in two main categories. The first is a vegetable based cold soup; the other is a fruit based. In these categories, seasonal vegetables and seasonal fruits are featured.

When making the cold soup, it is difficult to hide an inferior flavor so you want to make sure you use the best, well ripened, unbruised fruits or vegetables. In winter you can have your hot tomato soup and grilled cheese; now you can cool it down and have chilled tomato with grilled cheese Panini. (Just try some and see what you think. Let me know.) Cold soups need to have a strong flavor or the favor can get lost in the chilling.

Some soups can be served either hot or cold, but you need to be aware of the consistency. If it has been thickened to serve hot, you might need to thin it with milk, wine or broth a bit to be served cold.

Most chilled soups are delicious and very refreshing. They can be prepared in advance and don't have to be reheated. Now understand, just because it is a chilled soup, doesn't mean you can't serve it in the cooler months. You are the master of your kitchen, serve what you like when you like. There are not those strict rules that my generation seem to create and live by. Experiment and try many different cold soups recipes. Find the few that you really like and have fun with them. You can always experiment and add just your own spices and ideas.

# Fruit Soups

Fruit soups are a great way to enjoy the summer meal. Seasonal berries or stone fruit soups are traditional in Scandinavia and Eastern Europe. In Scandinavia the fruit soup is called 'Fruktsoppa' (old fashioned fruit soup). In this soup (dessert) you will find dried apricot, dried cherries, and other dried fruits and nuts. Sometimes they are served before the meal, but most times after and are considered as soup/dessert.

The fruit soups are a balance of sweet and tart. They are accented with a touch of wine and cream or sour cream. Also fresh lemon can be used to add to the flavor of the fruit. Garnish the fruit soups with a piece of the fruit itself and a dollop of sour cream. I have enjoyed the few I have in this book, but there are many more kinds of fruit soups. Cold soups have become much more popular over the last twenty years. Again, they can be used at lunch or dinner, before the meal or as dessert after the meal.

Experiment, take your favorite fruit and add it to one of these recipes. Instead of cherries, make it peach soup. Add a taste of Peach Schnapps' to perk it up. You can add mint to most or use a different white wine.

I have found that many men have put their noses up when they hear about cold soups. But give them a taste and they can turn around quickly and enjoy it. I have to say that it is much more fun to serve any of these cold soups at a ladies' luncheon which always seems to tempt their taste buds.

Honey Dew Soup with mint and lime© Connie Hope

# Blueberry Soup with Wine

**2 cups water**
**1 Tablespoon cornstarch**
**2 ½ to 2 ¾ cups fresh blueberries,**
**3 Tablespoons sugar**
**1 ½ cups  wine  ***
**½ cup sour cream or plain yogurt**

Wire whisk cornstarch with ¼ cup water.
Combine blueberries, cornstarch, water, sugar, and wine.
Cook low heat until blueberries are soft (15-20 minutes).
Put in food processor and blend until berries are smooth.
Chill overnight in refrigerator.
Serve with a dollop of sour cream or yogurt.
Serves 2-3

*Here are some ideas for wines in the Blueberry soup:

1 ½ cups Marsala wine
Or
1 ¼ cups grape juice
1 teaspoon brandy
Or
1 ¼ cups dry white wine
1 teaspoon brandy
Or
¾ cup sherry
¾ cup sweet vermouth

Blueberry Soup with Wine © Connie Hope

# Cold Melon Soup

**2 ripe cantaloupes**
**¼ cup dry sherry**
**6 sprigs of fresh tarragon**
**Salt and pepper to taste**

Cut melon in half.
In a cheesecloth over a bowl, put seeds and juice and strain.
Scoop out flesh in melon*.
Put melon in a food processor, juice from seeds, tarragon
  and dry sherry. Puree until smooth.
Add salt and pepper to taste.
Chill for several hours  and serve in bowls with sprigs of
    fresh tarragon as garnishing.
Serves 3-4

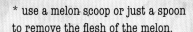

* use a melon scoop or just a spoon to remove the flesh of the melon.

Cold Melon Soup © Connie Hope

# Cold Strawberry Soup

1 quart strawberry yogurt (about 4   8 oz containers)
1 cup milk
¼ teaspoon cinnamon
1 pint fresh strawberries, cleaned and sliced
1  (8 oz) container plain yogurt for garnishing.
Dash of nutmeg
Lemon slices or strawberry for garnish

Puree strawberries in food processor.
Combine strawberry yogurt, milk, cinnamon and strawberry
        puree.
Chill for several hours.
Serve with a dollop of plain yogurt and a dash of nutmeg.
Place one lemon slice or strawberry on top.
Serves 4

Strawberries © Connie Hope

# Cold Strawberry Soup with Wine

1 quart fresh strawberries, cleaned and sliced
½ cup fresh orange juice
¼ cup fresh lemon juice
¾ cup white wine
1 Tablespoon cornstarch
4 teaspoons of sour cream for garnishing
4 cut strawberries  as garnish

Combine berries, orange juice, lemon juice, and cornstarch
    in pot.
Cook over medium heat, stir continually.
Mixture will become somewhat clear and will thicken.
Let cool to room temperature then add wine and mix.
Chill in refrigerator for several hours until cool.
Garnish with dollop of sour cream and cut berry.
Serves 4

# History of Gazpacho Soup

The name Gazpacho soup derives from the Arabic word meaning literally 'soaked bread'. This popular cold soup has its origin from the Andalusia area of Spain and has influence from Greece and Rome, and Moors and Arab culture. Gazpacho is mostly served cold and is considered a peasant's soup or worker's broth. Hence these recipes were seldom written down, but merely passed on from family to family by word of mouth.

The original soup was a blend of stale bread, olive oil, garlic, some liquid, either water or vinegar or both. What- ever the seasonal vegetable or nut available was added to the mix. Gazpacho remains popular with field workers for lunch as a method to cool off during their work on hot summer days. This has evolved into other varieties, but the most popular is the tomato based, which is usually served cold. In addition to blended either by mortar or today with a food processor to puree the mixture, it is accompanied by different garnishes. The garnishes are usually the vegetables that are contained in the soup, chopped up and put on the top.

Mary Randolph from Virginia has been credited with the first known publication in the United States of Gazpacho soup. It is thought that Mary acquired these recipes by word of mouth from her sister who, at the time, lived for several years in Spain.

Today there are many variations of the original gazpacho. This is done by adding such things as avocado, cucumber, parsley, or watermelon just to name a few.

Gazpacho tastes better if made the day before serving, which allows for the flavors to blend. It is great served with crusty breads.
(1 and 2 below)

1. Wikipedia.org
2. Smith, Andrew F. Souper: Tomatoes: The Story of American's Favorite Foods, Rutgers  University Press, New Brunswick, NJ, 2000, page 68.

# Gazpacho (Cold)

6 ripe tomatoes, peeled and chopped
1 purple onion, chopped fine
1 cucumber, peeled, seeded, chopped
1 sweet red bell pepper remove seeds and chopped
3 stalks celery, chopped
2 Tablespoons fresh parsley, chopped
2 Tablespoons fresh chive, chopped
2 cloves minced garlic
¼ cup red wine vinegar
¼ cup olive oil
2-3 Tablespoons fresh squeezed lemon juice
2 teaspoons sugar
Tabasco sauce to taste
1 teaspoon Worcestershire sauce
4 cups tomato juice*
Salt and fresh pepper to taste

Combine all ingredients.
Mix if you like things chunky or puree in food processor.
Place in a tightly-sealed container in the refrigerator
   overnight to allow the flavors to blend.
Serves 4-6

# Gazpacho Soup    (variation)

1 14 oz can tomatoes
1 large green pepper
1 clove garlic
½ cup olive oil
3 Tablespoons lemon juice (fresh is best)
3 cups beef stock
1 small Spanish onion, chopped (purple onion)
1 cup cucumbers, peeled, diced
Salt and pepper to taste
Fresh, chopped 1/8 cup of any the following
   Chives
   Parsley
   Basil
   Chervil
   Tarragon
Or used dried, but not quite as much.

Add all ingredients together - leave it chunky or puree in
   food processor.
Paprika for topping and a dollop of sour cream or fresh
   pesto (see index) on top.
Refrigerate for several hours.
Serves 4-6

You can add so many different
spices to change the flavor:
Oregano
Thyme
Cilantro

*I also have used beef or clam
tomato juice for added flavor.

This is from my first cookbook,
*In Addition...to the Entrée.*

This is a quicker version by using
canned tomatoes rather than fresh.

Check out the pesto in the index or
use a jar of bought pesto for topping. Makes it interesting!

This can be made and cooked in a jiffy.

* There are different interesting types of canned corn, Mexicorn which has red and green peppers, Chipotle white corn which has hotter peppers. They would add more flavor and are fun to try.

** Use either Tabasco, or hotsauce

Variation:

Add 1 can (4 oz) green chilies
Or
Add 1/3 cup sherry or red wine
Or
Add 1 can (14 oz)diced
  tomatoes with green chilies.
Or
¼ of a bunch of cilantro
Or
2 Tablespoons cumin

# Black Bean Soup

1 can black beans, rinsed and drained
2 cups chicken broth (or use vegetable broth)
¾ cup chunky salsa, red
1 small (11 oz) can corn, drained*
Dash of some type of hot sauce **
2 teaspoons lime juice
Garnish:
1 cup shredded cheddar cheese
2 Tablespoons chopped green onion

Two methods to heat:

Microwave:
Combine first 5 ingredients in a large microwave bowl.
Cover and heat for 2-3 minutes or until mixture is heated
  throughout.
Put in serving bowls and add a little lime juice.
Garnish with cheese and green onion.
Serves 4-6.

Stove top:
Put first five ingredients in a pot and heat for 10-15 minutes
or until heated  throughout.
Put into individual bowls and add a little lime juice.
Garnish with cheese and green onion.
Serves 4-6

Black Bean Soup © Connie Hope

Black Bean Soup with corn © Connie Hope

# Black and White Bean Soup  (Vegan)

1 Tablespoon olive oil
1 onion, chopped
1 stalk celery, chopped
1 Tablespoon garlic, minced (1-2 cloves)
1 teaspoon thyme
1 can black beans, drained  (14.5 oz)
8 cups vegetable broth
1 teaspoon ground cumin
1 can white beans, drained (14.5 oz)
½ teaspoon dried sage
Garnish with vegan cheese

In a large pot, heat oil.  Add onion, celery, garlic and thyme
    and heat until celery is tender, 8-9 minutes.
Add black beans, 4 cups vegetable broth, and cumin to pot.
Stir in white beans and remaining broth and sage.
Bring to a gentle boil and then simmer for 30-40 minutes,
    stir occasionally. Garnish with cheese
Serves 6-8

# White Bean Soup

2 cups white beans*
6 cups chicken broth (or use vegetable broth)
1 small ham hock (Optional)
1 cup onions, minced
1 cup celery, chopped
½ cup leeks, minced
3 Tablespoons butter
3 sprigs parsley
1 thyme sprig
1 bay leaf   ( 3 items tied together)
Salt and pepper to taste
Dash cayenne
½ cup parsley minced for garnishing

Saute onions, celery, and leeks in butter, until they are soft.
Combine with beans, broth, ham hock, spices.
Cover and bring to a boil, then simmer for 2 hours.
Remove tied spices and ham hock.
Remove a little of the ham from the bone and add it to the soup.
Serve 6-8

White Bean Soup Chunky© Connie Hope

For a different flavor, substitute one cup of tomato juice for one cup of vegetable broth.

*White beans are Navy beans or pinto beans, or Cannellini beans.

White Bean Soup in the Pot© Connie Hope

Can also be pureed.

* Instead of the oil, you can substitute 2 slices of bacon, chopped.

** You can make this vegetarian by substituting vegetable broth for the chicken stock.

Variation:
- Add 3 cloves of garlic, minced and saute with leeks.

- Add 2-3 teaspoons fresh rosemary instead of the dill.

Leek Soup with Shitake Mushrooms  © Connie Hope

You can use other types of mushrooms if you don't care for shitake. Shitake mushrooms have a different taste and add a great deal to any dish.

# Leek and Potato Soup

3-4 large leeks, cut into thick slices to the green areas
2 Tablespoons olive oil *
2 celery stalks, chopped
8 cups chicken broth**
10-12 small red skinned potatoes, unpeeled, cleaned and cut in chunks
1 Tablespoon dill weed
Salt and pepper to taste
½ cup dry white wine (optional)
croutons for garnish

Wash and slice leeks.
In a soup pot, add oil and saute leeks until tender, not brown.
Add remaining ingredients except dill, salt and pepper and croutons.
Bring to a boil.
Reduce to medium and cook until potatoes are tender.
Puree in food processor or immersion blender.
Season with dill and salt and pepper.
Serve hot with croutons
Serves 6-8

# Leek Soup with Shitake Mushrooms

2 cloves garlic, minced
4 large leeks, cleaned, chopped using white and green parts
2 Tablespoons olive oil
1 ½ cups dry white wine
6 large potatoes, peeled, and cubed
6 cups vegetable broth (or chicken broth)
1 bay leaf
2 teaspoons dried thyme
Salt and pepper to taste
½ cup fresh parsley, chopped
2 cups shitake mushrooms, chopped

In soup pot, saute leeks, mushrooms and garlic in olive oil until tender.
Add wine, cook slowly until wine is reduced by 1/3.
Add potatoes, broth, bay leaf, thyme, salt and pepper.
Stir and simmer until potatoes are tender, about 30 minutes.
Serve with crusty bread and top with fresh parsley.
Serves 5-6

# Leek and Potato Soup (can serve hot or cold)

**3 Tablespoons butter (or margarine)**
**3 medium leeks**
**1 medium onion, chopped fine (about ½ cup)**
**3 medium potatoes, peeled and diced**
**1 quart chicken broth**
**1 cup heavy or light cream**
**2 Tablespoons chive chopped**
**Salt and pepper to taste**

In a large Dutch oven heat the butter and sauté the leeks and
    onions until tender not brown.
Add potatoes and broth.
Bring to a boil, cover and simmer until tender (20 minutes).
If you like pureed soups, put in a food processor and then
    return to Dutch oven.
If you prefer soups that are chunky, do not puree.
Add salt and pepper.
Bring to a boil and stir in cream, reheat but do not boil.
Sprinkle with chives.
Serves 5-6

Leek and Potato Soup © Connie Hope

# Sweet Potato Soup

**1 Tablespoon bacon fat**
**1 cup onions, chopped**
**2 ribs celery, chopped**
**1 pound sweet potatoes, peeled and diced**
**5 cups chicken broth**
**Salt and pepper to taste**
**½ teaspoon nutmeg (can add more)**
**Sour cream for top**

Sauté onion, celery, and sweet potatoes in bacon fat for 5
    minutes.
Add broth, cover and bring to a boil, simmer until tender.
Puree in blender and reheat.
Add salt and pepper, and nutmeg.
Serve with a dollop of sour cream on top.
Serves 5-6

Leeks © Connie Hope

Thanks, Mom
I have always loved this soup.

This has lots of great flavors with all the different spices and herbs.

For a different taste you can also add:
½ teaspoon sage
3 Tablespoons sherry

You can use an immersion blender and puree the soup, or leave it chunky.

# Spiced Carrot-Ginger Soup

1-2 Tablespoons olive oil
1 cup onions, chopped
½ cup green onions, chopped
4 cups carrots, chopped
3 cups potatoes, cleaned, peeled and cubed
2 Tablespoons fresh ginger, grated or chopped
¼ teaspoon curry powder
¼ teaspoon ground cinnamon
¼ teaspoon ground nutmeg
1/8 teaspoon ground cloves
Salt and pepper to taste
1 bay leaf
3 (15.5) cans chicken broth

Heat oil, add onions, and saute.
Add carrots and potatoes and cook for 1 minute.
Add ginger, and other herbs and spices and broth.
Bring to a boil, reduce heat and simmer for about 1 hour.
Discard bay leaf. Puree in food processor.
Return to pot and reheat. Serve with green onion.
Serves 6-7

# Split Pea Soup with Corned Beef

1 pound green split peas, dried
2 ½ quart stock from cooking corn beef.
3 onions, chopped
2 carrots, diced
Bay leaf
Parsley
Cayenne
Salt and pepper
1-1 ½ cups corned beef

Wash and drain peas.
Add all ingredients except corned beef and bring to a boil.
Reduce heat and simmer for 2 hours. Puree or leave chunky.
Return to pot, add corned beef and reheat for 20 minutes.
Serves 4-6.

# Squash & Carrot Soup

1 pound carrots-cleaned, peeled and cut into ½ inch slices
1 ½ pounds squash, peeled, seeded, cut into 1 inch cubes.
    ( You can use your favorite squash such as Acorn,
    Buttercup, Butternut or any others)
2 teaspoons of butter or margarine
½ cup finely chopped onions—use either white onion, or to
    give more color and a stronger taste, use a Bermuda
    (purple) onion
1 Tablespoon ginger root-minced
1 ¼ cups cream  (use either half and half or light cream)
1 cup chicken broth
2 teaspoons of grated orange zest
Salt & pepper to taste. I leave chunks of squash in soup.

Fill a soup pot with 2 inches of water.

Add carrots and bring to a boil, simmer for 10 minutes.

Add squash cubes, simmer 10 minutes. Drain and set aside.

Put squash and carrots in food processor and puree.

Melt butter in pot and put onions and ginger and sauté
    for 2-3 minutes until onions are tender .

Add carrots and squash in the pot with the onions.

Add the half and half, broth and orange peel.

Bring the mixture to almost a boil, but do not let it boil.

Reduce heat immediately—if electric, take off burner.

Soup can be served hot or cold.

Serves 3-4

# Cream of Cauliflower Soup

½ cup green onion, top only
2 Tablespoons butter
2 Tablespoons flour
Salt and pepper to taste
2 cups chicken broth
2 ¼ cups frozen cauliflowers, thawed and chopped
2 cups milk
1 ½ cups (6 oz)cheddar cheese, shredded
2 Tablespoons dry sherry, (Optional)
1 Tablespoon chives minced for garnish

In a soup pot, saute onion in butter until tender.

Stir in flour and salt and pepper until blended.

Add broth a little at a time.

Bring to a boil, stir for 1 minute or until thickened.

Reduce heat and add cauliflower, simmer for 3-5 minutes.

Add milk and cheese and stir until cheese is melted.

Stir in sherry. Garnish with chives.

Serves 4-6

The orange and ginger add a great exotic flavor to the soup.

You can put a dollop of pesto or sour cream to decorate the top of the soup.

It is a great soup to remove the chill in the fall air.

This is quick and easy.

Thanks, Mom. I really enjoyed this one.

# Potato and Mushroom Chowder

½ cup yellow onions, chopped
½ cup butter or margarine
2 Tablespoons flour
Salt and pepper to taste
3 cups vegetable broth (or other broth or water)
I pound mushrooms, sliced
I cup celery, chopped
I cup potatoes, peeled and diced
½ cup carrots, chopped
I cup light cream
¼ cup parmesan cheese, grated

In a soup pot, add butter and saute onion until tender.
Add flour, salt and pepper to taste.
Stir into a smooth paste. Gradually add vegetable broth.
Stir continually. Bring to a boil for 1-2 minutes.
Add mushroom, celery, potatoes and carrots.
Reduce heat and cover and simmer for 30-45 minutes.
Vegetables should be tender. Can be pureed.
Wire whisk cream gently into pot mixture.
Warm and serve with parmesan cheese on top.
Serves 4-5

# Roasted Squash Soup with Crispy Bacon

4 cups butternut squash, diced
2 large onions, sliced
3 Tablespoons olive oil
3 cups chicken broth
½ cup heavy cream
¼ cup bacon bits

Set oven to 425 degrees. Place squash and onion on a pan.
Add oil and toss to coat.
Bake 25 minutes until tender.
Put squash, broth, cream in a bowl and puree.
Put puree mix back in the soup pot.
Cook slowly for 15 minutes. Salt and pepper to taste.
Serve and garnish with bacon.
Serves 5-6

# Pinto Bean Soup

1 ¼ cup pinto beans, canned or dried
1 ham hock
6 cups chicken or pork broth
1 cup onions, chopped
½ cup celery, chopped
¼ cup leeks, chopped
¼ cup carrot, chopped
1 clove of garlic, minced
3 Tablespoons olive oil
1 can tomatoes  (28 oz)
1 bay leaf
Parsley sprigs
1 cup pasta, optional

Saute onion, celery, leeks, carrots and garlic in oil.
Add beans, ham hock, broth, tomatoes, spices, salt, pepper.
Bring to a boil, then simmer covered for 3-3 ½ hours.
Discard bay leaf and parsley sprigs.
Remove ham hock and cut any meat off.
Puree only 2 cups of soup and return all soup into pot and
    reheat.
Serves 6-8

# Parsnip Soup with Ginger

2 teaspoons olive oil
1 onion, chopped
1 leek, sliced thin
2 carrots, thinly sliced
1 ½ pounds parsnips, peeled and sliced
4 Tablespoons ginger, peeled and  grated
2-3 cloves of garlic, minced
6 cups vegetable broth
Zest from orange
1 cup orange juice
Salt and pepper to taste
Chives for garnishing

Heat the oil, add onion and leek, cook until soft, 5 minutes.
Add the carrots, parsnips, ginger, garlic, orange zest, broth,
    salt, and pepper. Simmer covered for 40-50 minutes.
Cool slightly, puree with immersion blender.
Return to pot and add orange juice.  Simmer for 15 minutes.
If too thick, add more vegetable broth, slowly.
Garnish with chives and serve.
Serves  5-6

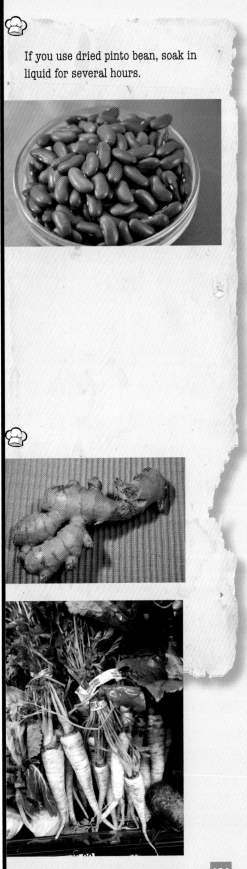

If you use dried pinto bean, soak in liquid for several hours.

*To ribbon a carrots:
Peel carrot.

Take the peeler and
holding the thickest end,
peel the carrot away
from you in ribbons.

**Any white bean that you like can
be used.

# Lemongrass Soup with Mushrooms and Tofu

4 cups chicken broth
1 inch piece of ginger, cut into strips
3 Tablespoons lemongrass (use from a jar or fresh from an
    Asian market, or use the tube of spices)
Thai chilies, stemmed and seeded  (I'd start with one and
    increase if you like the heat)
1 Tablespoon Thai fish sauce
½ block firm silken tofu, cut into small squares
Handful of fresh shiitake mushrooms, sliced (use any type
    of your favorite mushroom)
1 carrot, peeled
1-2 scallions, sliced
¼ cup bamboo shoots
½ bunch fresh cilantro, chopped

Combine ginger, lemongrass and chilies in a medium pot.
Add the broth and fish sauce and bring to a boil.
Reduce to a simmer and cover for about 25 minutes.
Strain all solid ingredients from stock.
Bring stock to boil, add mushrooms, tofu, and bamboo  shoots.
Let cook 10-15 minutes. Add lime juice.
Garnish with ribboned carrots*, or cilantro.
Serves 4-5

# Cheese Tortellini and Kale Soup

3-4 Italian sausage links, sliced
1 onion, finely chopped
1 cup fennel bulb, chopped
3-4 cloves of garlic, minced
1 ½ teaspoons fresh thyme, minced
½ teaspoon red pepper flakes
2 Tablespoons olive oil
2 boxes (32 oz) chicken broth
1 cup water
4 cups, fresh kale, chopped
1 can (15 oz) cannellini beans or navy beans rinsed and
    drained**
1 package (9 oz) cheese tortellini, refrigerated

In a large soup pot, cook the sausage, onion, fennel, garlic,
    thyme and pepper flakes in oil.
Sausage should not be pink, drain fat.
Add broth and water and bring to a boil.
Stir in kale and beans and bring to a boil.
Reduce heat and simmer until kale is tender.
Add tortellini and cook for another 10 minutes until tortellini is tender.
Serves 8

# Potato Soup with Arugula

2 Tablespoons olive oil
2 leeks, cleaned and chopped
4 medium potatoes, peeled and diced
3 cups chicken broth
1 cup baby arugula *
¼ cup heavy cream
2 teaspoons lemon juice
Salt and pepper to taste

Heat oil in a pot over medium heat.

Add the leeks and cook for at least 8 minutes.

Add the potatoes and cook for another 10 minutes or until
the potatoes are tender.

Add the broth.

Heat to a boil, reduce to low.

Cover and cook for 20 minutes.

Add arugula and cook for 1 minute.

Place  half mixture in blender and puree.

Or you can use an immersion blender which is much faster
and less clean up.

Repeat for the other half mixture.

Return pureed mixture to pot and cook over medium heat
until hot.

Salt and pepper to taste.

Stir in cream and lemon juice.

Serves 5-6

Potato Soup with Arugula pureed© Connie Hope

Leeks can be dirty inside.
Soak them in water for a few
minutes then clean in between
the leaves before cutting.

* You can also use escargot or
spinach. These items will turn
the soup a light green.

I also like this soup chunky.
Eliminate the immersion
blender part.

## Pumpkin Soup

½ cup onions, chopped
3 Tablespoons butter
2 cups mashed cooked pumpkin (or canned, 20 oz can is over 3 cups)
1 teaspoon salt
1 Tablespoon sugar
¼ teaspoon nutmeg
¼ teaspoon ground pepper
3 cups chicken broth
½ cup light cream (can substitute soy milk and a little flour to thicken )

Brown onions slowly in butter.
Put mashed pumpkin into the onion pan and add salt, sugar, nutmeg and pepper. If you prefer a smooth soup, puree in food processor.
Slowly add chicken broth, mixing with wire whisk.
Heat thoroughly. Do not boil.
Slowly add the cream and reheat.
Garnish with croutons and parsley.
Serves 4-5

This is a basic pumpkin soup recipe with a nice even and creamy taste.

This recipe is from In Addition... to the Entrée.

These soups can be served in a small, hollowed-out pumpkin. Cut off top of a small pumpkin down lower than usual. Save lid to keep soup warm. Use a melon baller to hollow out pumpkin to about ½ inch from skin.

©Connie Hope

## Spanish Pumpkin Soup

Add to the recipe of Pumpkin Soup
3 minced garlic cloves
1 ¼ cups cilantro, chopped
Do not use the ½ cup cream
Bread cubes fried in garlic olive oil
Cilantro sprigs

Put garlic in with the onions to brown.
Add cilantro with the chicken broth.
Heat and serve.
Garnish with croutons and cilantro.
Serves 4-5

Spanish pumpkin soup has a little more spice to the taste with the addition of the garlic and cilantro. It also is not as creamy as no milk or cream is added.

# Pumpkin-Leek Soup

2½ cups leeks, use mostly the white part, diced
1 medium cooked, mashed pumpkin (or 1 large can)
1 can chicken broth (10 ½ oz  or use 1 1/4  cups)
¼ cup heavy cream
1 teaspoon allspice, ground
½ teaspoon nutmeg, ground
½ teaspoon ginger, ground
¼ teaspoon cloves, ground (this can be optional if clove is
     something you don't care for)
¼ cup almonds (toasted or blanched)  (They are used for
     Garnishing, so I prefer them thinly sliced blanched, but
     your choice.)
1 teaspoon cinnamon, ground
2 Tablespoons oil (I usually use canola, but any will do.)
Salt and pepper to taste
Several spoonfuls of sour cream for garnish


In a large sauce pan medium heat, add the oil and leeks.
Sauté until tender. Stir in all spices, broth, and pumpkin.
Cover and reduce to a simmer.
Simmer for at least 20 minutes.  Stir occasionally.
Put mixture in a food processor or immersion blender.
Return the mixture to the sauce pan and heat.
Season with salt and pepper to taste.
Add heavy cream and warm until soup is heated thoroughly.
Garnish with sliced almonds, sour cream. Serves 3-4

Vegan  Option

Omit the heavy cream. You can replace with soy milk, but you will have to thicken
the milk a little with a mixture of 3 Tablespoons of flour and just enough water to
make a thick paste.  Make sure that you stir continually in the same direction with
the wire whisk.
Use Vegan sour cream for garnishing.

**Baked Pumpkin Seeds**
I worked with Eleanor and she gave
me this recipe. Thanks.

The hardest thing is to get the fiber
away from the seeds. Place seeds in
a strainer and run water over them.
Pull the seeds away from the fibers
with your hands.  It is slimy.
Heat oven to 350 degrees.
Put seeds on a paper towel for a few
minutes to remove extra moisture.
Spray a cookie sheet with nonstick
butter spray.
Put the seeds in a single layer on the
cookie sheet.
Sprinkle with salt.
Bake them for 10 minutes or until
golden. Turn and bake another 10
minutes.
Cool and store in an airtight container.

Variation:  Try additional seasonings
on your pumpkin seeds—either Cajun
seasoning, Worcestershire sauce, soy
sauce or garlic salt. These are some
of the many possibilities.

This is from *In Addition...to the
Entrée.*

This has just a nice spicy flavor to it.

On that cold day, it will warm you.

I also like to serve this soup in the pumpkin shell. I just hollow out the pumpkin and put hot water in for a few minutes. Then add the soup and bring it to the table. Everyone will love the presentation.

You can also buy soup tureens that look like a pumpkin.

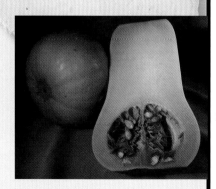

# Curried Pumpkin Soup

1/3 cup chopped onion
1 teaspoon minced garlic
1 teaspoon curry powder
2 Tablespoons butter or margarine
1 cup pureed fresh pumpkin ( or 15 oz can of pumpkin)
¼ teaspoon nutmeg
1/8 teaspoon allspice
2 cups vegetable broth (or use chicken broth)
1 ½ cups milk
1 bay leaf
1 Tablespoon cornstarch or arrow root or tapioca powder for
    thickening
2 Tablespoons heavy cream (optional)
Chopped chives for garnishing

In a large pot, cook onion, garlic and curry in the butter or
    margarine for a few minutes until onion is tender.
Add pumpkin, nutmeg, sugar and bay leaf.
Stir in broth and bring to a boil.
Reduce heat and simmer uncovered for 15 minutes.
Remove bay leaf.
Stir in 1 cup of milk, cook on low heat for few minutes.
In another bowl, stir together the remaining ½ cup milk and
    cornstarch until dissolved, then add to the pan.
Cook and stir until thickened. Cook two more minutes.
Garnish with a dollop of sour cream on the top.
Makes 4-6

# Curried Yellow Squash Soup

½ cup thinly sliced leek
1½ pounds yellow squash sliced thin (3)
4 cups water
1 teaspoon curry powder
1 teaspoon virgin olive oil
¼ teaspoon turmeric
Dot with sour cream and Chutney of your choice

In a large saucepan, cook leeks in oil slowly, stirring often
  until the leeks are soft and tender.
Add curry powder and turmeric, continue stirring mixture.
Add squash and water, then simmer. Check for tenderness.
It should cook at least 15 minutes. Cool mixture.
Put in blender or immersion blender and puree.
Season soup with salt and pepper.
Serve either chilled or hot.
Serves 4-5

# Creamy Artichoke Soup

2 Tablespoons olive oil
2 leeks, white part only, washed and chopped
1-2 cloves of garlic
1 potato, peeled and chopped
1 (8 oz) package frozen artichoke hearts, thawed*
   ( I have also used the cans of artichoke hearts)
2 cups chicken broth (or you can use vegetable broth)
Salt and pepper to taste
2 Tablespoons sour cream**
2 Tablespoons chopped chives for garnish

Heat oil, add leeks and garlic, and stir.
Add potato and cook for 5-7 minutes. Stir.
Add artichokes, broth, salt and pepper.
Cook medium, (vegetables should be tender) about 25 minutes.
Puree the soup using an immersion blender.
Add the 2 Tablespoons sour cream (or mascarpone cheese)
Blend.
Serves 4-5

Creamy Artichoke Soup ©Connie Hope

I really like garlic in my food, so I go for the larger amount of cloves, sometime adding one more clove. Your choice.

*If you use fresh, you just want to take the hearts. Make sure you cut out the thistle choke part and discard. That's why I use the frozen or canned. They've already done that.

** You can use mascarpone cheese in this recipe. Sometimes you can find it at a supermarket. If not, here is the recipe:

Yields 1 ½ cup

16 oz cream cheese, soften
1/3 cup sour cream
¼ cup whipping cream

Mix together until smooth.

The photo is without the cream added or blended. I like it really chunky.

We went out to dinner the other night and the restaurant served this soup. It was really good, so I did some checking and found a few of the recipes.

# Spinach Artichoke Soup

### For the Soup

1 teaspoon olive oil
2 shallots, chopped
1-2 cloves of garlic, minced
2 cups artichoke hearts (canned or frozen)
2 cups spinach leaves
2 teaspoons dried basil
1 teaspoon dried oregano
4 cups vegetable broth
Salt and pepper to taste

In a soup pot, heat oil, add shallots and garlic and saute.
Add artichokes, basil, oregano and saute for 3-4 minutes.
Add the spinach, vegetable broth and mix well.
Bring to boil. Simmer for 10-15 minutes until spinach is cooked down.
Serves 4

Spinach Artichoke Soup © Connie Hope

If you want it creamy, you can do this.

### For the Cream
1 can white beans(great northern or navy), rinsed and drained
1 cup milk (almond milk adds a great deal)
4 Tablespoons lemon juice (fresh is best)

Combine ingredients for the cream and use an immersion
  blender until smooth.
Put cream and mix together, simmer 10 minutes.
Serves 4-5

# Bean and Sausage Soup

2-3 Tablespoons olive oil
1 ½ pounds sweet or hot Italian sausage, in casing, sliced
1 medium onion, chopped
2 medium carrots, peeled and diced
2 medium stalks of celery, diced
2 cloves of garlic
1 can (14 ½ oz ) diced tomatoes (optional)
4 (15 ½ oz) cans of Great Northern Beans*
4 cups chicken broth
Salt and pepper to taste

In a large pot, put oil and saute sausage until brown on all
    sides, about 5 minutes.
Add onions, carrots, celery, garlic and herbs until browned
    slightly.
In a small bowl, mash either with a fork or a potato masher,
    one can of the beans.
Add broth, tomatoes (optional) ,mashed and whole beans,
    salt, pepper and sausage.
Cover and simmer for 20-30 minutes.


# White Bean and Escarole Soup

2-3 Tablespoons olive oil
3 oz ham diced
½ cup onion, diced  *
3-4 cloves of garlic, minced
1 teaspoon fresh thyme **
¼ teaspoon cayenne pepper or red pepper flakes
1 head escarole, washed, trimmed and chopped
2 (15 oz) can cannellini beans, drained and rinsed
1 cup chopped or diced whole tomatoes
5 cups chicken broth
Salt and pepper to taste

Heat oil in large soup pot, add ham, and saute for 4-5
    minutes.
Remove meat and set aside.
Add onion and saute until golden.
Add, garlic, thyme,( or rosemary) cayenne pepper, and saute
    for 2-3 minutes.
Add the escarole, and stir until wilted, about 3 minutes.
Add beans, tomatoes, broth, and salt and pepper to taste.
Bring to a boil, then lower heat immediately and simmer
    for 20 minutes.  Serve hot.
Serves 5-6

* You can substitute other types of
beans.  Try butter beans or pinto
beans or your choice.


** Herbs that can be used:

1 Tablespoon fresh minced basil or
1 teaspoon dried basil
or
1 Tablespoon fresh thyme or 1
teaspoon dried thyme
or
1 Tablespoon fresh marjoram or 1
teaspoon dried marjoram.
or
your choice

* Substitute ½ cup leeks instead of
onions.

** You can also substitute 1 teaspoon  fresh rosemary instead of
the thyme.

# Vegetable Bean Soup

3 medium carrots, sliced
1 ½ cups onions, chopped
1 cup celery, sliced
1 Tablespoon olive oil
2-4 cloves garlic, minced
1 (32 oz) box of chicken broth
2 (15 oz) cans navy or great northern beans, drained, rinsed
2 cups fresh broccoli, florets only
Salt and pepper to taste
½ teaspoon dried rosemary
¼ teaspoon dried thyme
1 cup fresh baby spinach

In oil, saute carrots, onions and celery until tender.
Add garlic, cook 2-3 minutes longer.
Stir in broth.
Add one can of beans, broccoli and seasonings.
Bring to a boil, reduce and simmer 5-7 minutes.
The second can of beans, put in a bowl and use an
     immersion blender. Add to the soup mix with the
     spinach. Simmer 5 minutes, until spinach and pureed
     beans are heated. Serves 7-8

# Roast Cauliflower Soup with Curry and Ginger

1 head cauliflower, separated into flowerets
2 large parsnips, peeled and thickly sliced
2-3 Tablespoons olive oil
1 large onion, sliced (about 2 cups)
6 cups Chicken Broth
1/3 bunch fresh cilantro, chopped
1 Tablespoon fresh ginger, minced
½ teaspoon curry powder
½ teaspoon ground cumin
½ cup yogurt
Garnish with bacon or cilantro

Heat oven to 425 degrees. Place cauliflower and parsnips in
  a roasting pan.
Pour 1-2 Tablespoon oil over vegetables. Toss to coat. Bake
  30 minutes.
Heat remaining oil in a soup pot. Add onions, cook until
  tender.
Add broth, cilantro, ginger, curry, cumin, cauliflower mix.
Bring to boil, reduce to low, and cook 25 minutes.
Stir in yogurt. Use an immersion blender. Return to pot and heat. Garnish with
crumbled bacon or cilantro. Serves 5-6

# Connie's Cooking Tips for Cold Soups

## Some Garnishing for Soups

- Croutons are always tasty in soups. You can buy them in many different flavors.

- Chopped chives are also very eye appealing on top of chilled soups. Also try parsley sprigs, mint sprigs, rosemary, and basil leaves, or any other herb leaf in your garden. It is easy to pick one of the spices in the recipe and just accent with it.

- A great idea is to put mint leaves, or rosemary or dill leaves in ice cube trays. But you want them in the middle. Here's how. Boil some water, then let it cool for a few minutes. Fill the ice cube tray half fill and put the leaves in it. Place in freezer and let freeze, then take out and fill tray the remaining way up. When you serve your cold soup, place one or two ice cubes in the chilled soup as a garnish.

- Heavy cream can make a neat pattern on the top of the bowl of soup as a garnish for cold or even hot soups. I like these on Chilled Cherry soup, which is a pink shade or a darker pea soup or cucumber soup. Here are several patterns to try:

1. Using a teaspoon, drip cream on top of the bowl of soup. Form a circle with the drops. Then take a small sharp blade knife and go through each drop to create a circle, which should look like hearts. You may need to practice this several times before you bring it out to your guests.

2. Place a Tablespoon of cream on the surface of the bowl of soup. Draw the small sharp knife away from the center of the circle to make an even pattern, which will resemble curved spokes.

Experiment and try other patterns.

- Sometimes leeks have grit in and on them. Place the sliced leeks in a bowl of cold water and swish them around a bit. Lift and place in a colander to drain. Hence, leaving any grit in the water and not on your leeks to be used in soup.

# Stew

*'I would like to find a stew that will give me heartburn immediately, instead of at three o'clock in the morning'* John Barrymore

What is the difference between a soup and stew? The Internet describes the stew as a "dish containing meat, vegetables and a thick soup-like broth made from a combination of the stewing liquid and the natural juices of the food being stewed." Stews are similar to soups, and in some cases there may not be a clear distinction between the two. Generally, stews have less liquid than soups, are much thicker, and require longer cooking over low heat. While soups are almost always served in a bowl, stews may be thick enough to be served on a plate with the gravy as a sauce over the solid ingredients.

One of the most important differences between soups and stews is the thickness. A stew can be simply described as a 'hearty soup' with meats and vegetables, including potatoes, and is much thicker than a soup. A stew is usually considered a main dish rather than a first plate, which a soup is considered. The liquid in a stew is minimal and usually thickened to the point of being more than gravy.

Another different between soups and stews is that soups can be eaten as either hot or cold dishes. Fruit soups are almost like desserts. Stews, on the other hand, are basically a water base with just a few vegetables and are served hot.

The other difference is the cooking time. The flavor of a stew stems from the slow cooking process, the natural flavoring of the foods simmered in the water or juices. Sometimes a thickening agent is added to make the broth more like thick gravy. Soups rely on added flavorings such as condiments and garnishes, while stews just go with the basic vegetable and meat flavor with little added flavor. But this is not always 'written in stone'.

Beef Barley Stew © Connie Hope

# Brunswick Stew

4-5 chicken breasts (I use boneless) or chicken parts
8 cups of chicken broth
Salt and pepper to taste
1 (10 oz )package frozen or canned  baby lima beans
2 large onions, diced
3 cloves of garlic, minced
1  large can tomatoes
1 ½ cups diced potatoes
2 cups sliced okra
4 cups whole kernel corn, drained
Salt and pepper to taste
1 Tablespoon sugar

Place chicken parts in a Dutch oven, add broth and salt ,
    cover and simmer for about 2 ½ hours. (or I have used a
    crock pot and cooked it for 6 hours, stirring occasionally.)
Remove chicken and remove meat from bones.  Set aside.
Skim fat from broth.
Add remaining ingredients except chicken, cover and
    simmer for 1 hour.
Add chicken, salt, pepper and heat for 2-5 minutes.
Serve with crusty bread or rolls.
Serves 7-8

Brunswick Stew © Connie Hope

When I was twelve, my family went to Williamsburg and one of the restaurants made this stew. It was wonderful, so I asked if I could have the recipe.

© Okra by Connie Hope

Okra really adds a lot to this stew.  If you've never tried it, now is the time.

Variations:
I added ¼ teaspoon cumin
¼ teaspoon basil, dried

© Connie Hope Brunswick Stew in Crock Pot

This is one of my favorites and it is so easy. I just love sweet potatoes and, with the chicken, it has a great flavor.

You can also put this in a slow cooker and cook for 5-6 hours.

* You can also use a can of lentils.

** You can use any squash. I've used butternut squash for this one.

*** This recipe can also be put into a crock pot. Cook for 7 hours on Low or 4 hours on High.

# Chicken and Sweet Potato Stew

6 chicken thighs, skin removed and fat trimmed
2 pounds sweet potatoes, peeled and cut in strips
½ cup mushrooms, sliced thin
6 large shallots, peeled and cut in half
4 garlic cloves, minced
1 cup chicken broth
1 cup white wine
2 teaspoons fresh rosemary, chopped (or ½ t dried rosemary)
2 Tablespoons wine vinegar
Salt and pepper to taste

Put all ingredients in a large soup pot with medium heat.
Stir occasionally for 5 minutes then lower heat.
Cook for 2 hours slowly.
Serves 6.

# Chicken and Squash Stew

1 ½ -2 pounds chicken breast, skinless and chunked
1-2 Tablespoons olive oil
2-3 cloves of garlic, minced
½ teaspoon cumin
½ teaspoon coriander
Salt and pepper to taste
¼ teaspoon cinnamon
1 ¼ cups dry brown lentils, rinsed and drained*
1 onion, cut in chunks
3 ½ cups chicken broth
1 cup water
1 large yellow summer squash, cut in chunks**
½ cup dried apricots
Sliced green onion (optional) garnish

In a bowl, combine chicken, garlic, cumin, coriander,
   cinnamon, toss to coat.
Add oil and heat chicken, browning.
In a soup pot, add water, broth, lentils, onion and chicken.
Cover and simmer for 1 hour. *** Add squash and apricots,
   cook for 40 minutes. Garnish.
Serves 5-6

# Turkey Vegetable Stew with Egg Noodles

6 cups of chicken broth (You can get turkey broth around
   Thanksgiving. I buy lots.)
2 turkey breasts, boneless and skinless, cubed
1 cup onions, chopped
2 cloves of garlic, minced
1 cup each celery and carrots, chopped
2 potatoes, peeled and cubed
2 bay leaves
Salt and pepper to taste.
¼ teaspoon dried marjoram
Optional:  oregano, thyme, sliced mushrooms
8 oz of egg noodles
2 Tablespoons fresh parsley, ends chopped

In a soup pot, combine broth, turkey pieces, onion,
   garlic, potatoes, celery, and bay leaves.
Salt and pepper to taste. Bring to a boil, simmer 30 minutes.
Bring to a boil, add egg noodles.  Cover and cook 6-8
   minute or until the noodles are just tender.
Stir in parsley, remove bay leaf. Serve in bowls for 4-5.

# Turkey Vegetable Stew another version

1 20 oz lean boneless turkey breasts and ½ cup flour
1 Tablespoon oil
2 cups fresh mushrooms, sliced
1 cup each carrots, and onions, chopped
½ cup celery, chopped
4-5 cloves of garlic, minced
1 cup dry white wine
1/2 cup tomato paste
1 Tablespoon fresh rosemary, chopped
¼ cup, fresh parsley, chopped
1 teaspoon lemon zest, grated

Cube turkey and toss in flour. In pot, heat oil at medium.
Cook turkey to well-done. Add all veggies, and garlic.
Cook until veggies are softened, about 5 minutes
Add wine, tomato paste, rosemary.  Bring to a boil.
Reduce to medium and simmer for 30 minutes or until
   veggies are tender, stirring occasionally. Then add zest.

This is quick and easy to make.


You can substitute
2 turkey burgers, cut into bite-size
pieces for turkey breast or pieces.

Again, this can be put in a crock pot for 7 hours Low or 4-5 hours on High.

# Hearty Turkey and Vegetable Stew

2 Tablespoons butter
2 turkey breasts, skinned, boneless, and cubed
¼ cup flour
2 onions, chopped
2 stalks of celery, chopped
2 carrots, peeled and ½ inch cut
2 potatoes, peeled and cubed
2 cups mushrooms, cleaned and chunked
2-3 cloves garlic, minced
1 green bell pepper, diced
1 can corn (optional)
¼ teaspoon dried marjoram
1 teaspoon rosemary
1 Bay leaf
3 cups chicken broth (turkey broth if you can find it)

Toss turkey in flour.
In a soup pot, add butter and cook and simmer turkey, until browned.
Remove and set aside.
Add onions, celery, carrots, potatoes, mushrooms, garlic, pepper, and simmer until tender, 5-10 minutes.
Add turkey, spices, broth and corn.
Cover, simmer and cook 1 to 1 ½ hours.
Remove bay leaf.
Serves 5-6

Hearty Turkey and Vegetable Stew © Connie Hope

# Beef Stew (Basic)

2 pounds boneless chuck roast or stewing meat
3 Tablespoon olive oil
Salt and pepper to taste
3 yellow onions, cut into chunks
½ cup flour in a bowl
3 cloves garlic, minced
I cup red wine (optional)*
3 cups beef broth
½ teaspoon dried rosemary (or fresh)
I bay leaf
½ teaspoon dried thyme (or fresh)
4 carrots, peeled, cut into I inch slices
2 stalks celery, cut into I inch slices
3 large russet potatoes, peeled and quartered**
¼ cup fresh parsley, chopped
Several sprigs fresh parsley for garnish

Put the meat cubes in the bowl with the flour and coat them.
In large pot, heat olive oil, add beef cubes and brown.
Add salt and pepper to meat.
Once meat cubes are browned, remove from pot with a slotted
    spoon and set aside. Add onions and saute until tender.
Reduce heat to low, add remaining flour, wire whisk it.
Add garlic and cook for several more minutes.
Add the wine and wire whisk the pan; get any little
    pieces stuck to the pot. This will start to thicken.
Simmer for about 5 minutes, then add broth, bay leaf,
    thyme, rosemary, parsley and beef.
Cover and cook low for I hour. Remove bay leaf.
Add potatoes, carrots, celery.
Cover and simmer 30 minutes or until vegetables are tender.
If too thick, add a little beef broth. Add salt, pepper to taste.
Allow to set for about 15-20 minutes covered, then serve.
Serve with crusty bread.
Serves 6-8

*If you eliminate the cup of wine, then add 1 cup of beef broth. The wine adds a great deal of flavor. Something to consider

Remember if you won't drink the wine, don't use it in cooking.

** You can substitute new potatoes for the russets potatoes or half and half with sweet potatoes.

Beef stew is very flexible in the ingredients. I use what I have in my refrigerator or freezer. If you have some carrots cooked, add them or extra rice . Or maybe you have some squash or peas, so add them. It is great for using leftovers.

Beef Stew © Connie Hope

These are just a few of the things you can add.

Use you imagination and add something that your family likes.

Or clean out veggies in the refrigerator and add them.

Experiment!

# Beef Stew variations:

You can add some of these items or only one to the stew. Your choice.

- 1/3 cup barley
- 1 cup green beans
- 1 cup  peas
- 1 cup lima beans
- 2 cups diced turnips
- 1 pound mushrooms, discard stems and slice thick
- 1 pound portabella mushrooms, sliced thick
- 1-2 cups chunked sweet potatoes
- 1 Tablespoon Worcestershire sauce
- Omit the cup of red wine and substitute 1 can of beer and ½ teaspoon paprika
- 1 can (14.5 oz) diced tomatoes
- Omit the ½ teaspoon rosemary and substitute ½ teaspoon marjoram
- Put beef cubes in a low dish and pour some additional wine over it.  Cover with plastic and refrigerate for 12-24 hours.

Beef Stew © Connie Hope

# Beef and Barley Stew

2 Tablespoons olive oil
3 pounds beef, cubed
Salt and pepper to taste
1 cup flour in bowl or plate
1 white onion, diced
3-4 stalks celery, chopped in ½ inch pieces
3 cloves garlic, minced
1 (32 oz) carton beef broth (4 cups)
4 potatoes, peeled and cubed
1 Tablespoon Worcestershire sauce
1 teaspoon paprika and thyme
2 teaspoons marjoram
1 can tomato paste
1 (14 oz ) can diced tomatoes
1 pound mushrooms
1 package frozen green beans (or canned)
4-5 large carrots, chopped in ½ inch pieces
1 cup barley
Extra water or beef broth if needed
½ cup fresh parsley for top
Noodles or rice (optional)

Combine flour, paprika, salt and pepper in plastic bag and
   coat beef.
Brown beef cubes in olive oil, remove cubes from pot.
Saute celery, garlic and onions briefly.
Add broth and wire whisk pan to remove meat pieces.
Return beef cubes, add spices and potatoes.
Add carrots, sliced mushrooms, green beans, diced tomatoes,
   and tomato paste.  Simmer for 1 ½ hour.
Add barley and simmer very slowly for 1 more hour.
Chop parsley and add to top.
Can serve with noodles or rice.
Serves 8-10

Variations:
1 cup green peas
2 cups turnips

Beef and Barley Stew©Connie Hope

Additions:

¼ teaspoon marjoram
Or ½ teaspoon basil.

1 Tablespoon Worcestershire sauce.

1 pound of mushrooms

* Bundle the spices with a string.

** You can use regular salt or sea salt.

Tomato Paste in Tube

* or leave them chunked

# Beef Stew with Beer

2 Tablespoons olive oil
I cup onions, chopped
2 medium carrots, chopped
2 pounds beef, cut into I inch cubes
I can or bottle of beer
2 cups beef broth
Salt and pepper to taste
4 medium potatoes, peeled and quartered
½ teaspoon thyme, dried
I bay leaf

In a soup pot, add olive oil, onions, carrots and cook until
    translucent, about 5-7 minutes.
Stir in beef cubes and quickly brown on all sides.
Add beer, beef broth, salt, pepper, potatoes, thyme, bay leaf.
Bring to a boil, reduce heat and simmer slowly for 2 hours.
Beef should be tender. Remove bay leaf.
If more liquid is needed, add beef broth.
 Serves 6

# Beef Stew with Sweet Potatoes

3-4 medium size sweet potatoes, chunked
4 sage leaves, fresh*
2 sprigs of thyme*
I sprig rosemary*
4 pieces bacon, cut in ½ inch strips
I ½ pounds stewing beef, cut in I inch chunks
Salt and pepper to taste**
4 cups beef broth or chicken broth
2 cups onions, diced
I cup carrots, I inch sliced
I cup celery, I inch sliced
I Tablespoon tomato paste (for small amounts, use a tube)
5-6 cloves of garlic, minced
2 Tablespoons butter
Parsley leaves for garnish

Bake sweet potatoes in the microwave (6-8 minutes)
    or in the oven 400 for 40 minutes.
Heat large pot and cook the bacon until crisp.
Transfer bacon to paper towel. Save I T fat in pot.
Brown the beef on all sides in pot. 5-7 minutes.
Add broth, onions, carrots, celery, paste, garlic and herbs.
Bring to a boil, then reduce to simmer, cover for I hour.
Uncover and cook at low simmer until all veggies are tender.
Scoop out flesh from sweet potato and place in blender with
    I cup of the stewing liquid and butter until smooth.*
Add to stew, stir well and simmer for 5-8 minutes. Remove herb bundle
and garnish with parsley.
Serve 6.

# Beef Burgundy (Beef Stew)

3 pound boneless beef cut into 1 inch cubes
1 bottle dry red wine*
5 slices bacon, cut into ½ inch pieces
2 Tablespoons olive oil
2-3 cloves of garlic, minced
1 onion, chunked
1 Tablespoon lemon juice (fresh is best)
1 teaspoon Worcestershire sauce
1 Tablespoon tomato paste**
2 bay leaves, dried
Salt and pepper to taste
1/8 teaspoon allspice, ground
½ teaspoon paprika
3 cups beef broth
6 carrots, peeled and in 1 inch cubes
1 pound small white onions
6 potatoes, peeled and cubed
1 pound mushrooms, sliced
Egg noodles, cooked
Crusty bread
Parsley for garnish

The day before pour wine in bowl, add beef cubes, cover.
Refrigerate for 24 hours. Pat beef dry with paper towel.
In soup pot, cook bacon until brown, put on paper towel.
Add oil, and add marinated beef cubes and saute until brown.
Remove beef to a plate. Add garlic and onion saute until soft.
Stir wine marinade, lemon juice, bay leaves, salt, allspice,
    Worcestershire sauce, tomato paste, pepper, and paprika.
Add bacon and browned beef cubes. Add enough hot beef
       broth to cover meat.
Cover and simmer for 2-3 hours, stirring occasionally.
Remove bay leaves, Add carrots, onions, potatoes, and
       mushrooms, Simmer for 30-40 minutes, until vegetables
       and meat are tender. Heat noodles and serve.
Serve with crusty bread.
Serves 6-8

Beef Burgundy © Connie Hope

I use either Pinot Noir or Montepulciano.

Again, if you don't drink it, don't use it.

** I use the tomato paste
in a tube. It can be reused
and refrigerated

If you are adding wine to a recipe, make sure it is wine that you would drink.

Serve with crusty bread.

Variation:
Add
3 medium carrots, cut in ¼ inch slices
Add after cooked for 1 ½ hours.

Or 2 potatoes chunked
Or 2 teaspoons fresh oregano
Or 2 teaspoons fresh thyme

Have fun and experiment.

# Beef and Butternut Squash Stew

3 Tablespoons olive oil
I onion, diced
2-3 cloves of garlic, minced
I Tablespoon fresh rosemary, minced
I Tablespoon fresh thyme, minced
2-2 ½ pounds of stew beef, cut into 1 inch chucks
Salt and pepper to taste
I cup red wine
I pound butternut squash, peeled, cut into 1 inch chucks
¼ cup sun-dried tomatoes
3-4 cups beef broth
2 Tablespoons parsley, chopped leaves

In a soup pot, heat 3 Tablespoons of olive oil.
Add onions, garlic, rosemary, thyme, saute until tender,
    about 3-4 minutes on medium heat.
Add the beef and brown on all sides, about 5-7 minutes.
Add wine and stir until the browning in the pan is mixed in.
Add the squash, sun-dried tomatoes, and beef broth to cover
    the beef and squash.
Bring to boil, then reduce and simmer covered for 1 hour.
Salt and pepper, sprinkle with chopped parsley.
Serves 6

# Lamb Stew

I pound lamp, cubed
½ cup flour
2 Tablespoons olive oil
I clove garlic, chopped
2 large leeks thin sliced (about 2-2 ½ cups)
I large onion, thinly sliced.
I sweet potato, chunked
1-2 Tablespoons parsley, minced
I teaspoon paprika
½ lemon, juiced
Salt and pepper to taste
I cup vegetable broth
I package frozen artichokes  or I can
Mashed potatoes—either dried or fresh mashed (optional)

Coat lamb in flour on all four sides.
In a pot, saute lamb in oil until brown on all sides.
Add garlic, potatoes, onion, parsley and paprika.
Then add lemon juice, salt and pepper and broth.
Cover and simmer for 1 ½-2 hours.
Add the artichokes and cook another 20 minutes.
Serve hot with mashed potatoes. (optional)
Serves 4-6

# Goulash

2 pounds ground beef (you can use turkey if you prefer)
2 large onions, chopped
3-4 cloves garlic, minced
3 cups water (you can use beef broth )
2  cans (15 oz) tomato sauce
2 cans (14.5 oz) diced tomatoes
3 Tablespoons soy sauce
2 Tablespoons dried Italian herb seasoning *
3 Bay leaves
Salt and pepper to taste
2 cups  uncooked elbow macaroni (or your choice)

In a large pot, medium heat, brown the ground beef, stirring.
Break up ground beef as you stir for about 10 minutes.
Skim off some of the excess fat, stir in onions and garlic.
Cook until onions are translucent, about 10-12 minutes.
Stir in water, (or beef broth) tomato sauce, diced tomatoes,
    soy sauce, Italian seasoning, bay leaves, salt and pepper.
Bring mixture to a boil, then reduce to low, cover and simmer
    for 30-40 minutes, stirring occasionally.
Stir in the macaroni, cover and simmer until pasta is tender
    25-30 minutes, stirring occasionally.
Remove from stove, remove bay leaves.
Serves 4-6

# Hungarian Goulash

2 pounds top round beef, cut into 1 inch pieces
1 cup onions, chopped
3-4 cloves garlic, minced
2 Tablespoons flour
1 Tablespoon paprika
Salt and pepper to taste
¼ teaspoon dried thyme
1 can  (28 oz) whole tomatoes, undrained, chopped
2 cups beef broth (can use more)
3 carrots, peeled and cut in 1 inch pieces
1 bay leaf
1 cup sour cream for topping
Warmed cooked butter egg noodles

Combine beef, onion, and garlic in a large pot.
In a small bowl, combine flour, paprika, salt, pepper and
    thyme, mix well and add to meat mixture.
Add tomatoes with liquid, broth, carrots and bay leaf.
Cover and simmer for 1 hour or until carrots are tender.
Remove bay leaf and serve over noodles with sour cream.
Serves 4-5

*Gourmet Garden tubes make a very tasty Italian herb seasoning.  You can use this.

Variation:

½ green bell pepper, chopped
½ pound mushrooms, quartered
½ cup mozzarella cheese for topping.

For a Tex Mex Goulash
Add 1 cup corn
1 ½ teaspoons cumin
1 teaspoon chilies powder

Can be made in a crock pot or slow cooker.
High for 5 hours; Low for 8 hours

Oyster Stew is much like a soup, yet it is called a stew.

* White sauce
  3 Tablespoons of melted butter, 3 Tablespoons of flour and 1 cup milk. Melt butter, medium heat, then add flour while continually stirring with wire whisk, then slowly add milk and wire whisk. Set aside until ready for thickener.

**Poaching Oysters
2 cups water or liquid from oysters
12-18 shucked oysters, drained

In saucepan, bring water, to a simmer. Add oysters; simmer (Do not boil) until oysters begin to curl around the edges and become plump and firm, 1-5 minutes, depending on size of oysters. Drain oysters.

# Oyster Stew

12-18 fresh oysters (small ones are more tender)
2 cups light cream
2 cups milk
3 Tablespoon butter or margarine
Salt and pepper to taste
Pinch of dried thyme ( or use fresh sprigs of thyme)
Pinch of dried marjoram
White sauce for thickener *

Poach oysters** in their own liquid for 1-5 minutes.
In a pot, add light cream, milk, butter and seasonings.
Add oysters and simmer until warm.
Add slowly the white sauce and stir.
You will need to judge how thick you want the stew.
Add half of white sauce, stir and determine if thick enough.
Serves 4-5

# Oyster Stew with Vegetables

12-18 fresh oysters
3 potatoes, cubed
2-3 stalks of celery, diced
1 medium yellow onion, diced
2 cups half and half
2 cups milk
1 cup chicken broth
2 Tablespoon freshly chopped parsley
Salt and pepper to taste
¼ teaspoon thyme
Pinch of garlic powder
¼ cup of cornstarch for thickener (optional)

Saute diced vegetables and spice in chicken broth.
Add milk and half and half.
Heat until warm. Do not boil.
Stir in drained oysters and simmer for 25-30 minutes
Add cornstarch slowly continually stirring to desired
    thickness. If it is thick enough, do not add more.
Serves 4-5

Oyster Stew with Vegetables © Connie Hope

## Oyster Stew Quick and Easy

1 or 2 cans oysters
Salt and pepper to taste
¼ cup onion, diced fine
1 Tablespoon Worcestershire sauce
6 cups milk
1 Tablespoon butter

In a medium soup pot, add the milk, oysters, salt, pepper,
    onions, and Worcestershire sauce.
Bring to a slow boil, then simmer until onions are tender.
Add butter and allow to melt.
Serve with oyster crackers.
Serves 4-5

## Oyster Stew—richer

2-3 green onions, chopped
2 Tablespoons butter
12 oz fresh raw oysters, undrained
4 cups half and half
Salt and pepper to taste
1 Tablespoon fresh parsley
1/8 teaspoon cayenne pepper
Oyster crackers

Saute onions in soup pot in butter until tender.
Add remaining ingredients.
Cook over low heat until edges of oysters begin to curl.
Serve with sliced green onions and oyster crackers, garnish.
Serves 4-5

Oyster Stew is a favorite of
mine. I have included several
different ways to cook it.

Perfect for a special dinner.
It's quick and easy, but rich and filling.

"Serve with crusty bread.

This is similar to oyster stew.

You can always add your own favorite spices.
¼ teaspoon thyme
Or
¼ teaspoon basil.

Variations:
If you'd like a little thicker, add 4 Tablespoons instant mashed potatoes with the cream.

# Lobster Stew

2 lobsters, cooked (or about 4 cups of meat); you can use lobster tail or frozen pieces of lobster.
4-6 Tablespoons of butter
2 Tablespoons of green onion, chopped
4 cups milk
2 cups heavy cream
Salt and pepper to taste
1 teaspoon of paprika
¼ cup dry sherry (or use white wine)
Fresh sprigs of parsley for garnish
3 cups of cooked rice, optional

Remove the shells and cube meat.
In a soup pot, saute very slowly butter, green onions and lobster meat until light brown.
Add milk, and heat slowly for 15 minutes.
Add cream, bring just to a boil, then lower for 10 minutes.
Add salt and pepper and paprika.  Stir for 5 minutes.
Add dry sherry and heat for another 2-3 minutes.
Can be served with some rice in a bowl and the stew on top.
Serves 6-8

# Shrimp Stew

½ cup celery, chopped
½ cup onions, chopped
1-2 cloves garlic, minced
¼ cup butter
1/3 cup flour
Salt and pepper to taste
½ teaspoon dried thyme
1 can (14 ½ oz) diced tomatoes
2 cups chicken broth
1 to 1 ½ cups sliced cooked okra
Dash of hot pepper sauce
1 can (8 oz) minced clams, undrained
1 pound medium shrimp, shelled and deveined
3 cups cooked rice

In skillet medium heat, melt butter.
Saute celery, onions, and garlic.
Stir in flour, salt and pepper and thyme.
Cook and stir frequently for 10 minutes.
Stir tomatoes, chicken broth, clams, liquid and pepper sauce.
Cook for 5 minutes. Add okra, shrimp and cook 5 minutes more.
Add rice in a bowl and ladle shrimp stew on top.
Serves 6

# Fish Stew

3-4 cloves garlic, minced
2 medium onions, chopped
2 Tablespoon olive oil
1 (28 oz) can crushed or diced tomatoes
6 cups fish broth (or use water and 'Better than Bouillon')
½ cup fresh parsley, chopped
½ cup fresh cilantro, chopped
2 Tablespoons Worcestershire sauce
1 teaspoon cinnamon
1 teaspoon paprika
Salt and pepper to taste
1 ½ pounds cod fish or other white fish, cubed*
½ cup small pasta ( I use ditalini or small shells)

In a soup pot, saute in olive oil, garlic and onions for 5
    minutes.
Add tomatoes, fish broth, parsley, cilantro and bring to a
    boil.
Reduce heat to low and simmer for 15 minutes.
Add Worcestershire sauce, cinnamon, paprika, and fish.
Simmer for 10 minutes.
Add pasta and simmer for 8-10 minutes or until pasta is tender.
Salt and pepper to taste.
Serves 6

*You can use any white fish or even a combination of different white fish is great. We go fishing in the Gulf and catch snook. It's a great fish and I have used it in this stew.

'Better than Bouillon' in Fish Broth

Similar to Shrimp and Crab Gumbo with the addition of sausage and oysters.

Fish Broth

# Seafood Gumbo

1 pound lump crabmeat, fresh or canned
3 pounds medium raw shrimp
6 Tablespoons oil, divided
2 pounds frozen sliced okra, thawed (unless you can find fresh)
1 pound sausage, thinly sliced
2 Tablespoons flour
2 cups onion, finely chopped
1 cup celery, finely chopped
1 cup green pepper, finely chopped
3-4 cloves garlic, minced
1 cup green onions, chopped and divided
1 can tomato paste ( 6 oz)
3 bay leaves
1 teaspoon fresh thyme, finely chopped
1 teaspoon hot sauce such as Tabasco
Salt and pepper to taste
1 Tablespoon Worcestershire sauce
1 can  (14.5 oz) whole tomatoes, drained and coarsely chopped, reserve liquid
1 pint oysters (about 2-3 dozens)
¼ cup parsley, finely chopped
Cooked long grain rice

Pick crab meat, removing bits of shell if using fresh, or use crab meat from a can.
Remove shrimp shells. Refrigerate shrimp and crab.
Place head and shells in a large stock pot.
Add 8 cups water, salt and pepper.
Bring to a boil, then reduce and simmer for 1 hour.
Cool for 30 plus minutes, then pour stock through a strainer and reserve for later.  Discard shells and bits.
Heat 2 Tablespoons oil in a large skillet over medium heat.
Add okra and saute 10-12 minutes. Set aside.
Clean skillet and add 2 Tablespoons of oil.
Saute sausage until browned, about 8-10 minutes. Set aside.
Heat remaining oil in a large soup pot.
Add flour and stir, then reduce to medium heat.
Add onion, celery, pepper and saute 5 minutes or until vegetables are softened.
Add garlic and ½ cup green onions and cook for 3-4 minutes.
Stir in tomato paste and bay leaves, thyme, Tabasco, and Worcestershire sauce.
Stir in tomatoes and 1/3 cup of the tomato liquid.
Gradually stir in shrimp stock.
Add sausage and okra.
Bring to a boil and then cover and simmer for 30-40 minutes.
Stir in shrimp and remaining green onion.
Simmer for 5 minutes. Stir in crabmeat, oyster, and parsley.
Simmer for several minutes or until oysters are done.
Add salt and pepper to taste. Serve over rice.
Serves 6-8.

# Seafood Stew

3 Tablespoons olive oil
1 ½ cups onions, chopped
2 cups white potatoes, diced small
2 cups fennel, chopped
Salt and pepper to taste
2 cups white wine
1 can (28 oz) plum tomatoes, chopped
1 quart seafood (fish) stock*
3-4 cloves of garlic, minced
1 teaspoon saffron
1 pound shrimp, shelled and deveined
1 pound each halibut and bass fillets, cut into chunks
24 mussels, cleaned
1 teaspoon grated orange zest
Toasted baguette sliced and buttered as garnishing

Heat the oil in a soup pot.
Add the onions, potatoes, fennel, salt and pepper and saute
    over medium heat for 15 minutes until onions are brown.
Add wine, and scrap up the brown pieces (with a wooden
    spoon) that are at the bottom of the pot.
Add tomatoes and their juice, stock, garlic and saffron.
Bring to a boil, then reduce the heat and simmer for 20
    minutes or until the potatoes are tender.
Add the shrimp, fish, and mussels and bring to a boil, then
    lower to medium, cover and cook for 5 minutes.
Turn off the heat, but allow the pot to sit covered for at least
    another 5 minutes. The steam will soften the fish and
    open the mussels. Discard any unopened mussels
The fish and shrimp should be cooked. Add the orange zest. Salt &
pepper. Serve with the baguette.
Serves 6.

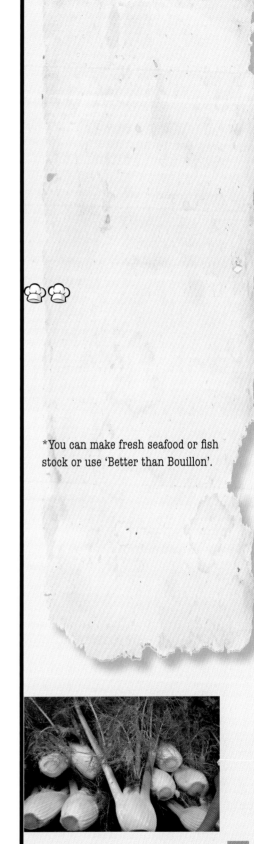

*You can make fresh seafood or fish
stock or use 'Better than Bouillon'.

My partner, Hewitt, goes fishing in Venice with his friend. We call him Dickless (Dick White). Anyway, they catch all types of fish and never a great amount of anyone kind. So, Dickless makes Bouillabaisse stew (soup) with all these different type of fish. His recipe is really rich with many fish and very tasty.

Thanks Dickless, for the addition to my new cookbook.

Options:
¼ teaspoon fennel seeds
2 teaspoons fresh parsley

Instead of the Spanish or red onion, try a Vidalia onion.

# Bouillabaisse
## (some called it a stew and some call it a soup)

Bouillabaisse is a French seafood stew (some call it a soup, but it is so thick, stew fits it better). It is made with various kinds of cooked fish, shellfish, and vegetables that are flavored with herbs and spices. Tradition states that there should be at least five (5) different fish in a bouillabaisse. In Marseille, which is the home of the bouillabaisse, they use at least seven (7) fish, that doesn't count the shellfish. Bouillabaisse gains rich flavor from vegetables such as onion, tomatoes, leeks and celery which are boiled and added to the stew. But it is the herbs and spices that give bouillabaisse its wonderful aromatic flavor. Some herbs and spices used are garlic, bay leaf, fennel, orange peel, and saffron. They are combined in the stew. What is nice in modern day, many different types of fish can be used.

1 cup butter
1 cup each squash, zucchini, tomatoes, leeks, carrots,
    Spanish onions, celery, fennel and stewed tomatoes,
    diced
1 -2 cloves garlic, minced (more if you love garlic, like me)
¼ cup olive oil
1 teaspoon saffron
1 teaspoon thyme
2 bay leaves
6 clams with shell
1 lobster tail, spit and cut into bite size pieces
4 large scallops, cut in half
4 large shrimp, peeled and deveined
½ pound fish (can use many different kinds)
½ cup white wine (optional)
1 quart fish stock( purchased or homemade)
Salt and pepper to taste

Saute onions, celery, carrots, leeks and fennel in olive oil on
    high heat for two minutes.
Add garlic, squash, zucchini and bay leaves.
Saute on medium high heat for two minutes.
Add pureed and stewed tomatoes, saffron, and fish stock
    and simmer for 10 minutes. Set aside.
On high heat in a large pan, brown the butter and add
    clams, lobster tails, scallops, shrimp and any fish used.
Stirring constantly, lightly brown the seafood.
Add the wine, fish stock mix, cover and simmer for 3-5 minutes.
Add salt and pepper to taste.
Serve with French bread.
Serves 6-8.

# Bean Stew

1 large can baked beans, don't drain
1 medium can lima beans, don't drain
1 medium can kidney beans, don't drained
1/2 lb hamburger
1/2 lb bacon
1/2 tsp. garlic powder
1 medium onion
1/2 cup catsup
1/4 cup yellow mustard
3 T cider vinegar
1/4 cup brown sugar
1/4 cup white sugar

Brown hamburger with garlic powder.
Cook bacon until crisp.  Crumble bacon.
Put meats in casserole dish. Add all ingredients and stir well.
Bake at 350 degrees for about 45 minutes. Serve 4-6

# Sausage and Lima Bean Stew

1 pound  dried lima beans (soak as per instruction on label)
1 pound pork sausage (either bulk or cut sausage casing and
　　use loose)
½ pound cubed cooked ham
½ cup onions
1-2 garlic cloves, minced
1 can condensed golden mushroom soup
2-3 Tablespoons ketchup (or use opened spaghetti sauce)
1 bay leaf

Rinse lima beans, put into pot and cover with water.
Bring to a boil, then reduce and simmer for 1 ½ hours.
Drain, reserve 2 cups liquid. Put 1 ½ cups liquid back in pot.
In skillet combine sausage, ham, onions, garlic and brown.
Drain off excess fat.
Add sausage mix to lima mix in soup pot.
Stir in 1/2 cup reserve liquid, soup, ketchup, and bay leaf.
Cover, simmer for 30-40 minutes. Remove bay leaf.
Serves 6

This is one of Bill's favorite recipes.
I worked with him and he just loved
to cook and bake.
Thanks, Bill

I found that I needed to add some
beef broth to keep it moist. Your
call.

Can also be prepared in a crock pot
after meats have been pre-cooked.

To cut fresh parsley,
I use scissors and snip off the
florets into a small container.

# Kielbasa Stew

1 pound Kielbasa sausage, cut into 1 inch pieces (you can also use turkey Kielbasa sausage)
1 Tablespoon butter
1 can (14 oz) beef broth or 2 cubes and 2 cups of water)*
1 can tomato soup
1 ½ cup water
3 cups shredded cabbage
1 onion, chopped
½ cup green peppers, diced
Salt and pepper to taste
¼ cup sour cream

In a large soup pot, add butter and brown sausage all sides.
Then add broth, tomato soup and water. Stir.
Mix in cabbage, onion, and bell pepper.
Salt and pepper to taste.
Bring to a boil, then reduce heat and simmer for 1 hour.
Stir in sour cream and heat for 3 minutes.
Serves 6

Kielbasa Stew © Connie Hope

# Lentil and Ham Stew

2 ½ - 3 cups ham, diced
2 cups lentils, dried
2 cups carrots, chopped
2 cups celery, chopped
1 cup onions, chopped
1 clove garlic, minced
6 cups chicken broth (or vegetable broth)
1 teaspoon oregano, dried
Salt and pepper to taste
1 16 oz frozen spinach leaves
2 Tablespoons lemon juice (use reamer for fresh juice)

Put all ingredients in a soup pot and cook slowly for 2 hours
    or until lentils are tender.
Stir in spinach, cover and cook another 15 minutes.
Stir in lemon juice.
Serves 4-6

# Three Sister Stew

1 Tablespoon olive oil
1 large onion, yellow, sliced
1 clove garlic, minced
1 jalapeno chili, finely chopped
4 cups yellow summer squash, diced (optional)
4 cups green zucchini, diced (optional)
4 cups butternut squash, peeled and cubed
3 cups green beans, cut 1 inch long pieces
1 cup corn, ( canned or frozen)
1 teaspoon dried thyme leaves, fresh would be 2-3
    teaspoons)
1 (16 oz) can either kidney beans or pinot beans  undrained

In a soup pot, heat oil and  saute onion, garlic and jalapeño
    chili for 2-3 minutes stirring occasionally.
Onion should be translucent.
Add remaining ingredients and cook for 10-15 minutes or
    until vegetables are tender.
Serve with crusty bread.
Serves 5-6

# Calico Beans Stew

1 ½ pounds hamburger meat
½ cup onions, chopped
2 Tablespoons olive oil
1 (15. oz)can kidney beans, drained
1 (14.5 oz) can lima beans, drained
1 (14.5 oz) can pork and beans
1 cup ketchup
1/4 cup brown sugar
Salt and pepper to taste
2 Tablespoons vinegar
2 cups beef broth
1 teaspoon dry mustard ( regular jar mustard)

Brown the meat and onions in oil in a frying pan for around
    5 minutes.
Put beans, ketchup, sugars, salt, pepper, vinegar and
    mustard in a soup pot.
Add beef broth. You may need a little more broth as it
    cooks.
Cook for one hour and a half at low heat. Stir.
Serves 6

Three Sister's Stew (variation)
Eliminate dried thyme

Substitute:
1 Tablespoon ground
    cumin seeds
2 Tablespoons fresh
    cilantro, chopped

See Three Sister's Soup for history
of the Three Sister's.  page  105

I like to use Rice Vinegar.

## Basic Chili

3 Tablespoons oil
2 medium onions, diced
1 medium red bell pepper, diced
5-6 cloves of garlic, minced
¼ cup chili powder (or use package of chili powder)
1 Tablespoon ground cumin
2 pounds ground beef ( or ground turkey)
Salt and pepper to taste
1can (28 oz) diced tomatoes
1 can (14 oz ) tomato sauce
2 cans (15 oz each) kidney beans, drained and rinsed*
¼ cup chopped jalapenos or green chilies, drained**
Shredded cheese, sour cream and scallions for garnishing

Put oil in a large soup pot and add ground beef, spices and
  vegetables, simmer, for 10-15 minutes, skim fat if any.
Add tomatoes, and beans. Simmer 1 hour. Serves 5-6.

## White Chili

1 pound turkey or chicken ground meat
1 medium onion, chopped
1-2 cloves garlic,  minced
1 Tablespoon olive oil
2 cans Great Northern beans (15 ½ oz each)
1 box or can chicken broth  ( 14 ½ oz box or can)
2 cans green chilies, chopped ( 4 oz each)
Salt and pepper to taste
1 teaspoon oregano, and basil and cumin
1/4 teaspoon cayenne pepper
1 cup sour cream ( 8 oz)
½ cup heavy cream

In a soup pot, saute turkey or chicken, onion, garlic in oil.
Add beans, chilies and seasonings.
Bring to a boil, then reduce and simmer for 40-50 minutes.
Stir in sour cream and heavy cream.
Reheat to serving temperature.   Serves 5-6.

White Chili © Connie Hope

# Chili with a Little Heat

1 Tablespoon olive oil
1 pound ground turkey or ground beef
1 medium onion, chopped
1 green pepper, chopped
1-2 cloves of garlic, minced
1 can diced tomatoes
2 celery stalks, chopped
1 can kidney beans, rinsed and drained (either the light or
    the dark beans)
1 small can chick peas rinsed and drained (optional)
1 can  (29 oz) tomato puree *
1 jalapeno pepper, de-veined, seeds removed, chopped if
    you like
2 Tablespoons chili powder
1 teaspoon thyme, oregano and rosemary
1 Tablespoon cumin
1 beef cube dissolved in ½ cup water
1 teaspoon cayenne pepper (optional)
2 Tablespoons Worcestershire sauce
1 Tablespoon basil
Salt and pepper to taste
Shredded cheddar cheese for topping (optional)
1 Tablespoon onion, chopped for each bowl (garnish
    optional)

In a soup pot, cook ground turkey or ground beef, onions,
    green peppers, celery, and garlic, medium heat with a
    little olive oil.
Drain any excess fat.
Add beans, tomatoes, tomato puree, chili powder, cumin,
    beef cubes, Worcestershire sauce and other species.
Bring to a boil, and reduce to a simmer.
Cook for 30-45 minutes or until you reach the desired
    thickness.
Serve in bowls with shredded cheddar cheese on top
Serves 4-6  Next day it's even better.

Chili © Connie Hope

* If you prefer very chunky chili, use another can of diced tomatoes in place of the tomato puree.

Variations: Use any one or more.

- Add 2 Tablespoons brown sugar, 1 Tablespoon instant coffee, and 1 Tablespoon baking cocoa
- Add 1 can (15 oz) black beans, drained and rinsed
- Add 1 can (15oz) garbanzo beans drained
- Add 1 can pork and beans
- Add 1 Tablespoon cumin
- Add 1 can (15 oz) corn, drained
- Add 1 cup chunky salsa either red or verde
- Add 1 can sliced olives, drained
- Add 1 can Great Northern beans, drained
- Add ½ pound sausage, fried, cut in 1 inch pieces and drained

Chili is something that you need to fit to your taste. Anything goes.  I have added a few green beans, some turkey sausage or any vegetable. Experimenting is the name of the game.

* Or you can use 'Better than Bouillon', 1 Tablespoon in a cup of water. You can also use vegetable bouillon to be vegan.

# Creamy White Chili-no meat

1 pound dried navy beans
1 onion, chopped
2-3 cloves of garlic, minced
1 Tablespoon olive oil
1 (10 ¼) oz can cream of chicken soup, undiluted
1 (10 ¼ oz) can cream of celery soup undiluted
1 cup water
1 potato, peeled and cubed
1 Tablespoon chili powder
1 teaspoon chicken bouillon granules*
Salt and pepper to taste
1 ½ cups half and half
1 (15 oz) can garbanzo beans (or chick peas)
    rinsed and drained

Put navy beans in a soup pot and add water to cover.
Bring to a boil and boil for 3 minutes.
Remove and cover and let stand for at least 1 hour.
Drain, rinse, and discard liquid.
Return beans to the soup pot and bring to a boil, then simmer
    for 45-50 minutes or until beans are tender.
Drain and discard liquid, then set beans aside.
In oil in the soup pot, saute onion and garlic until tender.
To soup pot add 1 cup water, potato, chili powder, bouillon,
    salt and pepper.
Cover and cook low for 15 minutes.
Add soups, cream, garbanzo beans and navy beans.
Cook for 15-20 minutes or until heated. Do not boil.
Top with parsley or cilantro flakes.
Serve 6-8

Creamy White Chili-no meat © Connie Hope

## Crock Pot verses a Slow Cooker
## Are they the same?

I thought a crock pot and a slow cooker were indeed, the same, but after some research I found there are many similarities, as well as several differences. Let's check this out.

Crock pots and slow cookers have three (3) things in common—a pot, a glass lid and a heating element.

A crock pot has only two settings 'Low' and 'High'. There can also be a 'Keep Warm' setting. The pot is ceramic or porcelain and round or oval. It has a glass lid and heating element that the pot fits into snugly.

A slow cooker has a hot plate that a metal pot sits on and has many different temperature settings, usually from one (1) to five (5).

In a crock pot the heating element surrounds the entire pot—bottom and sides—and heats continuously. The slow cooking heats from the bottom on cycles.

The result of both is a great dish that has cooked over many hours with little supervision. The outcome is a great tasting meal.

When I was talking to a friend about my cookbook, she said to me, 'You need to put lots of crock pot recipes in your book. I use a crock pot at least four times a week. You must have some new and fun crock pot recipes, so I can buy your book.' I thought on that for a while.

At the time I didn't have any crock pot recipes in my cookbook, nor did I have a crock pot. When I moved to Florida, I thought I wouldn't need it. So it's because of her that I went out and bought a crock pot and started making all the recipes that are now in this cookbook.

Thanks for the advice. I hope you enjoy them all. I have also put notes on the side panel if I found similar recipes that could be adapted to the crock pot.

Make it Fast
Cook it Slow

Crock Pot © Connie Hope

Picture of a slow cooker

* Italian seasoning can be home-made:

2 T Basil
2 T Marjoram
2 T Oregano
2 T Rosemary
2 T Thyme
Additional can be added
1 T Sage
1 T Cilantro

Mix together and store in an air tight jar.

Or you can use the tube of Italian seasoning.

# Minestrone Soup in a Crockpot

1 can (14.5 oz) diced tomatoes
2 cups carrots, diced
2 cups potatoes, diced
1 ½ cups celery, diced
1 sweet onion, diced
3-4 cloves garlic, minced
1 Tablespoon Italian seasoning *
Salt and pepper to taste
2 Bay leaves (optional)
4 cups vegetable broth
2 cups water
3 cups Tomato Juice (Clamato or V8 are good)
1 can (15 oz) red kidney beans (drained and rinsed)
1 can (15 oz) Cannellini beans,(drained and rinsed)
1 ½ cups zucchini, diced
1 cup small pasta
1 can (15 oz) green beans, drained (Sometimes I just add the green bean liquid to the soup)
Shredded cheese for garnish

Place first 9 ingredients in the crock pot.
Add the vegetable broth, water and tomato juice.
Cover and cook on Low for 6-8 hours or High for 3-4 hours.
After cooking time is up, add the kidney beans, cannellini beans, zucchini, green beans and pasta.
Cook on High for at least 30 minutes until pasta and veggies are tender.
Serve with thick crusted bread.
Serves 5-6 plus.

Minestrone Soup in a Crockpot © Connie Hope

# Jambalaya in a Crock Pot

1 pound chicken breast, boneless, skinless, & cut into1 inch
  cubes
1 pound sausage, sliced
1 can (28 oz) diced tomatoes, with juice
1 onion, chopped
1 green pepper, chopped
1 cup celery, chopped
2 cups chicken broth
2 teaspoons dried oregano
2 teaspoons dried parsley
2 teaspoons Cajun seasoning
1 teaspoon cayenne pepper
½ teaspoon dried thyme
1 pound frozen cooked shrimp, no tails

In a crock pot, mix chicken, sausage, tomatoes with juice,
    onion, green pepper, celery, and broth.
Season with oregano, parsley, Cajun seasoning, cayenne
    pepper and thyme.
Cover and cook on High for 4 hours or Low for 8 hours.
Stir in the shrimp during the last 30 minutes.
 Serves 4-5

Jambalaya © Connie Hope

# Chicken Tortilla Soup in Crock Pot

Cooking spray
1 ½ pounds chicken, boneless and skinless
2 cups frozen Southwest mixed vegetables *
1 can (10 oz) diced tomatoes
1 can Green chilies, undrained (around 4 oz)
1 Tablespoon ground chipotle chili pepper (optional)
1 ½ teaspoons cumin
4 cups chicken broth
¼ cup fresh lime juice
Cilantro and tortilla chips for garnishing

Spray crock pot. Place chicken, frozen vegetables, tomatoes,
   chili peppers, cumin and broth in crock pot.
Cover and cook Low for 6-8 hours.
Remove chicken and cut into strips and return to crock pot.
Stir in lime juice.  Reheat for 30 minutes.
Serve with tortilla chips and cilantro.
Serve 5-6

## Sausage Stew w/ Beans and Pasta in Crock Pot

1 onion, cut in chunks
2-3 carrots, chopped
4-5 cloves garlic, minced
8 oz dried, white beans  (cannellini, navy or others)
8 sprigs of fresh thyme, tied
1 pound sweet or hot Italian sausage, cut in 1 inch pieces
1 can, (14.5 oz) diced tomatoes
3 cups beef broth or chicken broth
2 cups water or use more broth
1 chunk Parmesan rind, about 4 oz.(optional)
½ cup ditalini pasta (or other small pasta)
2 Tablespoons chopped parsley (tops only)
2 teaspoons balsamic vinegar
Salt and pepper to taste
Crusty bread to serve with stew

Spread onions at the bottom of the crock pot.
Add carrots, garlic, white beans, thyme bundle and
    sausage links on top.
Add tomatoes, water or broth and pour over sausages.
Add the Parmesan rind.
Cook on High for 4-5 hours or Low for 8 hours.
Make sure beans are tender.
Remove the thyme bundle and the Parmesan rind.
Stir pasta into the stew and continue to cook, covered, for
    another 30 minutes.  Pasta should be done.
Stir in the parsley and vinegar.

Variations:

2-3 cloves of garlic, minced

½ cup celery, diced

## Ham and Potato Soup in Crock Pot

7 cups potatoes, diced
1 onion, diced
1 large carrot, diced
2-3 cups ham diced
2 teaspoon parsley, dried
1 teaspoon thyme leaves, dried
Salt and pepper to taste
5 cups vegetable broth
1 cup milk
½ cup sour cream

Add diced potatoes, onions, carrot, ham, thyme, parsley, salt
    and pepper to crock pot.
Cook on Low 7 hours or High 3-4 hours.
Remove 2 to 3 cups of potatoes and carrot.
In a bowl mash, then return to crock pot.
Add milk, and sour cream and stir.
Serves 6-8

# Crock Pot Chili

½ pound pinto beans, dried*
3   14 ½ oz cans tomatoes
2 Tablespoons olive oil
2 ½ -3 pounds chopped meat, browned and drained**
2 peppers, chopped  (I use green and orange)
2 medium onions, chopped
3-4 cloves garlic, minced
4-5 Tablespoons chili powder (depending on your taste)
Salt and pepper to taste
2 teaspoons cumin
Sour cream and shredded cheddar cheese for garnish

Soften dried pinto beans (putting in water and boiling).
Drain all water from the beans and rinse.
In pan you cooked meat, put the onions, peppers, garlic.
Heat for 3-4 minutes, then transfer to the crock pot.
Put the rest of the ingredients in the crock pot and stir.
Cover, cook on Low for 8 hours or High for 5-6 hours.
Top with sour cream and cheese.
Serves 6-8

# Crock Pot Chili Variation

I pound ground chop meat
I cup onions, chopped
½ cup green pepper, chopped
¼ cup red wine*
I Tablespoon chili powder **
I teaspoon  cumin
1-2 cloves of garlic, minced
Salt and pepper to taste
I can (15 oz) kidney beans, drained
I can stewed tomatoes (you can use one with jalapeno
   peppers or add one jalapeno pepper for heat!***
Shredded cheese for garnishing

In a frying pan, cook ground beef until brown.
Add chopped onion, pepper, garlic, cumin and chili powder.
Cook until onions are tender, about 8 minutes.
Place meat mixture in crock pot, stir in beans & tomatoes.
Cover and cook for 4-5 hours on Low or 2-3 hours on High.
Serves 4-5

* You can use kidney beans or other dried beans. I like the change of the pinto beans in the chili or chick peas. Experiment!

** You can also use turkey chopped meat

When you are cooking in a crock pot, the times are not exact. If you wanted to cook this on Low for 10 hours you could. Just check and stir every once in a while. Or don't.

* Remember, if you won't drink the wine, don't cook with it!

** You can also use the pre-packed chili mix. McCormick makes a good one. Or any of them. Experiment.

***When using jalapeno peppers, re-move the seeds and the veins. It cuts the heat!

I like to add a little rice. I cook it first, then add the last 30 minutes.

* I use the 'Better than Bouillon' beef and mix with water, heating just a little helps it mix better. Or you can use cans or a box of beef broth.

** I have a Worcestershire sauce with Vidalia onion that is very tasty.

# Sausage Gumbo in a Crock Pot

3 cups chicken broth
3 cans diced tomatoes (14 ½ oz)
¾ cup flour
2 sausages, cut in ½ inch pieces, browned lightly
2 onions, chopped
2 green peppers, diced
4-5 stalks celery, cut in 1/2 inch pieces
3-4 carrots, cut in ½ inch pieces
1 teaspoon oregano, dried
1 teaspoon thyme, dried
½ teaspoon red pepper
2 cups cooked white rice (optional)

Combine chicken broth and cans of tomatoes in crock pot.
Add the flour and stir in.
Add sausage, onions, peppers, celery, carrots, oregano,
    thyme and red pepper and stir.
Cover, cook on Low for 8 hours or High for 4-5 hours.
Last 30 minutes add the cooked rice.
Serves 4-5

# Crockpot Beef Stew

2 pounds of beef stew meat cut into bite-sized pieces
1 onion, finely chopped
2-3 stakes of celery, sliced in 1 inch pieces
3-4 cloves of garlic, minced
1   6 oz can tomato paste
4 cups of beef broth*
2 Tablespoons Worcestershire sauce**
2 cups baby carrots
4-5 potatoes, cut in bite-sized pieces (about 3 cups)
Salt and pepper to taste
1 Tablespoon dried parsley (fresh is best)
1 teaspoon oregano
1 cup frozen or canned peas  including liquid (optional)
1 cup frozen or canned corn including liquid (optional)
1 cup frozen or canned green beans including liquid (optional)
¼  cup flour and ¼ cup water

Combine, beef, celery, carrots, onion, potatoes, salt and
    pepper, garlic, parsley, oregano, Worcestershire sauce,
    beef broth and tomato paste in the crock pot.
Cook on Low for 8-10 hours or High for 6-7 hours.
About 30-40 minutes before serving, mix flour and water
    together, pour into the crock, mixing well, then add
    cans of vegetables. If too thick, add the juices.
Serves 5-6

# Beef and Broccoli Crock Pot Stew

1 ½-2 pounds flank steak
3-4 cloves of garlic, minced
½ cup carrots, shredded
½ cup soy sauce
¼ cup white wine
1 teaspoon olive oil
1 teaspoon honey
1 teaspoon dried ginger
1 teaspoon red chili pepper flakes
½ Tablespoon peanut butter
3 Tablespoons brown sugar
2 cups frozen or fresh chopped broccoli
Salt and pepper to taste

Cut flank steak into small pieces.
Place in crock pot.
Mix all ingredients except broccoli into Crockpot.
Cover and cook on Low for 6-7 hour or High for 4-5 hours.
Last hour, stir in the broccoli, cover and cook 1 more hour.
Serve with rice.
Serves 5-6.

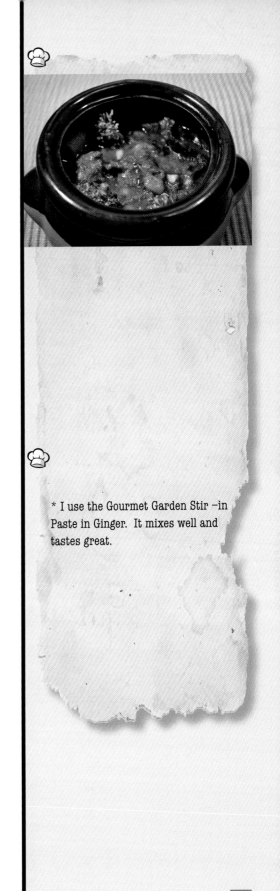

# Spicy Short Ribs in a Crock Pot

½ head cabbage, cut in half, then in quarters
1 cup carrots cut into 1 inch pieces
3-4 pounds of beef short ribs, fat trimmed
½ cup soy sauce
1/3 cup brown sugar
¼ cup rice vinegar
1 -2 cloves of garlic, minced
1 teaspoon ground ginger*
1 teaspoon oil (I like sesame oil, but you can use olive oil)
½ teaspoon crushed red pepper flakes
2 Tablespoons cornstarch
¼ cup water
¼ cup green onion, chopped for garnish

Place ribs in Crockpot.
Mix together soy sauce, sugar, vinegar, garlic, ginger, oil,
  red pepper. Pour over ribs. Carrots and cabbage on top.
Cook on Low for 7-8 hours or on High 5-6.
Transfer veggie to a bowl.
Skim the fat from the cooking liquid, discard.
Turn the Crockpot to high.
Whisk together the cornstarch and ¼ cup water.
Whisk in the liquid and cook until thick.
Spoon sauce over short ribs & vegetables.
Sprinkle w/ onion.
Serves 5-6.

* I use the Gourmet Garden Stir –in Paste in Ginger. It mixes well and tastes great.

* I add mushroom 'Better than Bouillon' to the water.

* If you won't drink it, don't use it.

# Crock Pot Cream of Mushroom Soup

½ cup butter
4 cups thinly sliced mushrooms
½ cup onion, finely chopped
½ cup flour
Salt and pepper to taste
¼ teaspoon nutmeg
4 cups water *
2 cups light cream
2 cups sour cream
I can (10 ¼ oz) chicken broth
½ cup parsley, chopped

Melt butter, add mushrooms, onions and saute 5-7 minutes.
Sprinkle flour, salt, pepper and nutmeg over vegetables.
Stir. Place in crock pot.
Whisk in water, cream sour cream and chicken broth.
Cover and cook on Low for 4 hours.
Turn to High and cook one hour longer.
Stir in parsley and serve.
Serves 5-6

# Cream of Mushroom Crock Pot Variation

½ cup butter
I onion, chopped
2-3 cloves garlic, minced
6 cups mushrooms, sliced
4 cups vegetable broth
I cup dry white wine*
I teaspoon tarragon, dried
Salt and pepper to taste
I cup heavy cream
¼ cup cornstarch

In a skillet, melt butter. Add onion and garlic.
Cook 4-5 minutes or until onions are translucent.
Add mushrooms and cook until tender.
Add wine, cook 3-4 minutes. Transfer to a crock pot.
Add vegetable broth, tarragon, salt and pepper.
Cover and cook on High for 2 hours or Low for 3-4 hours.
In a small bowl, whisk cream and cornstarch until smooth.
During last 30 minutes, stir in cream mixture until smooth.
Turn on High and cook until thickened.
Remove half of soup mixture with mushrooms. Use an
    immersion blender until smooth. Combine with other soup.
Serves 5-6.

# Creamy Tortellini Crockpot Soup

Jar of spaghetti sauce (24 oz)
2 cups water
¼ cup onion, diced
3-4 cloves of garlic, minced
½ cup carrots, diced
1 pound ground beef, browned
4 cups fresh spinach leaves, loosely packed
4 cups beef broth
8 oz cream cheese, cut into 1 inch cubes
8 oz fresh, sliced mushrooms
Cheese tortellini (16 oz  refrigerated or frozen)

Combine spaghetti sauce, water, meat browned, onions,
    garlic carrots, spinach, cream cheese, beef broth and
    mushrooms in a slow cooker.
Cook on Low for 7 hours or High for 5 hours.
When time is up, take a whisk to break up cream cheese.
Stir in the tortellini.
Cover and cook another 30-40 minutes or until tender.
If used frozen tortellini, cook another 40 minutes.
Serves 5-6

# Crockpot Irish Stew

1 ½-2 pounds cubed stew beef or lamb
1 can tomatoes, diced (14 oz)
1 can tomato sauce (8 oz)
2 cups carrots, sliced ½ inch thick
1 cup celery, sliced ½ inch thick
1 cup onion, sliced
¾ cup barley
5 cups beef broth
Salt and pepper to taste
1 bay leaf
½ teaspoon sage
½ teaspoon thyme

Combine all ingredients in a slow cooker.
Mix well. Cover, cook over Low heat for 7-8 hours.
May need to add 1 cup water or broth.
Serves 5-6.

This Irish stew has barley in it.

I only put a little of the jalapeno slices in this chili, but experimenting is the name of the game.

Salsa Verde has a wonderful flavor. I have used it even with scrambled eggs in the morning.

* I like to use the tube of tomato paste as it keeps well in the refrigerator for the next time needed. Or don't use it at all.

# Chicken Chile in a Crock Pot with Salsa Verde

4 chicken breasts, boneless and skinless
2 medium onions, chopped
2 medium green peppers, chopped
I cup pickled jalapeno slices (optional)
I (4 oz) can  chopped green chilies
2 (16 oz) jars salsa verde
2 (15 ½ oz) cans navy beans, rinsed and drained
I cup sour cream
½ cup fresh cilantro, minced
½ cup shredded cheese, sour cream and crushed tortilla chips

Put the chicken, onions, peppers, jalapenos and chilies in a
  crock pot.  Pour salsa verde over top.
Cover, cook on Low for 5-6 hours, chicken should be tender.
Remove chicken, cool a little so you can cube the chicken.
Return to crock pot, stir in beans, sour cream, and cilantro.
Heat for about 40 minutes.
Serve with topping.
Serves 5-6.

# Irish Stew in Crock Pot

2 Tablespoons of olive oil
I 1/2  pounds lean beef stew meat, cubed
2 Tablespoons flour
2 medium potatoes, peeled and diced
I (10 oz) package frozen carrots
½ onion, chunked
3 Tablespoons tomato paste*
3 cups beef broth
2 teaspoons Italian seasoning
1-2 cloves of garlic, minced
3 Tablespoons cornstarch
3 Tablespoons water
Salt and pepper

Heat oil in a fry pan, add meat and brown.
Then add flour and stir. Set aside.
Put potatoes, carrots, onion in the crock pot.
Then add the meat on top.
Combine tomato paste, beef broth, Italian seasonings and
  garlic and pour over meat and veggies.
Cook on Low for 6-8 hours, potatoes should be tender.
Combine cornstarch with water and make a paste.
30 minutes before stew is done, stir paste slowly into the pot.
Cook on high for 30 minutes, until the stew has thickened.
Add the salt and pepper and serve.
Serves 5-6.

# Nacho Grande Soup in Crockpot

1 pound ground beef
1 medium onion, diced  (I prefer sweet onion)
1-2 cloves garlic, minced
1 package (1 oz) taco seasoning
1 can condensed cheddar cheese soup (10 ½ oz)
1 can diced tomatoes and green chilies, (10 oz not drained)
1 ½ cups milk
1 cup shredded cheddar cheese
Tortilla chips, crushed for garnish
Other toppings such as chilies, or colored chips

In a skillet, cook ground beef, onion, and garlic until
    thoroughly cooked, then drain.
Spray crock pot with non-stick spray.
Place cooked meat mixture in crock pot.
Add taco seasoning, cheddar cheese soup, tomatoes, milk,
    and shredded cheese.
Stir well, cook Low for 3-4 hour.  Use a flat large bowl.
Top each bowl with crushed tortilla chips, shredded cheese
    and any other topping you might like.
Serves 5-6.

Really good and creamy soup.  The kids will love it.

# Mango and Coconut Chicken Soup for the Crock Pot

1 broiler chicken 3-4 pounds , remove skin, cut in bite size
    pieces
2 Tablespoons olive oil
1 can (15 oz) baby corn, drained
1 package (15 oz) frozen spinach, chopped and thawed
1 cup Edamame, frozen, shelled, and thawed
1 small red pepper, chopped
1 can(13.6 oz) light coconut milk
½ cup mango salsa
1 teaspoon fresh ginger root
1 medium mango, peeled and chopped
2 Tablespoons lime juice
2 green onions, chopped

In a skillet, brown chicken in oil.
Transfer chicken to a crock pot.
Add corn, spinach, Edamame and pepper.
In a small bowl, combine the coconut milk, salsa and ginger.
Pour mixture over vegetables.
Cover, cook on Low for 6-8 hours or until chicken is tender.
Just before serving, stir in mango and lime juice.
Sprinkle with green onions.
Serves 5-6

Mango adds an interesting flavor to the chicken soup

Home made mango salsa

# Pasta e Fagioli in Crock Pot

The other Pasta e Fagioli recipes uses ham. You can substitute the ground beef.

1 pound ground beef
1 large onion, chopped
1 box (32 oz) chicken broth
2 cans (14 ½ each) diced tomatoes, undrained
1 can (15 oz) white kidney beans or cannellini beans, rinsed
    and drained
2 medium carrots, chopped
1 ½ cups cabbage, finely chopped
1 large stalk celery, finely chopped
1 Tablespoon fresh basil ( 1 teaspoon dried)
2 cloves of garlic, minced
Salt and pepper to taste
1 cup ditalini or small pasta
Grated Parmesan cheese for garnish

In a large skillet, cook beef and onion until no longer pink,
    drain.
Transfer to crock pot.
Stir in broth, tomatoes, beans, carrots, cabbage, celery, basil,
    garlic, salt and pepper.
Cover and cook Low for 8 hours or High for 4-5 hours.
Stir in pasta cover and cook on High for 30 minutes or until
    tender.
Sprinkle with cheese to garnish.
Serves 6-8.

Pasta e Fagioloi in Crock Pot © Connie Hope

# Vegetarian Lentil Soup in a Crock Pot

3 cups vegetable broth
3 green onions, chopped
1 (10oz) can diced tomatoes with green chilies, undrained
1 cup mild salsa
1 cup dried lentils, rinsed
1 cup corn
1 (8oz) can tomato sauce
1 (4 oz) can green chilies, chopped
3-4 cloves of garlic, minced
1 teaspoon chili powder
1 teaspoon cumin
½ teaspoon celery salt
½ teaspoon paprika (optional)
¼ teaspoon cayenne pepper
1 (16 oz) package of firm tofu, drained, cut in cubes
1 (4 ¼ oz) can ripe olives, chopped for garnish
3 green onions, sliced  for garnish

Combine vegetable broth, onion, diced tomatoes, salsa,
    lentil, corn, tomato sauce, green chilies, garlic, chili
    powder, cumin, celery salt, paprika and cayenne pepper
    in the crock pot.
Cover and cook Low for 8 hours or until lentils are tender.
Serve in bowl, sprinkle with tofu, olives and green onion.
Serves 5-6.

Vegetarian Lentil Soup in a Crock Pot © Connie Hope

*I like the tomatoes with the basil
and green peppers.


* You can also make your own
tacos strips from tortillas.

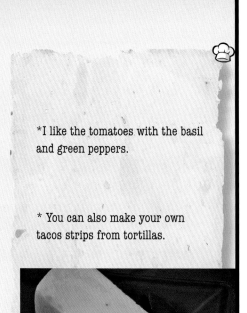

# Chicken Taco Soup in a Crock Pot

2 cups corn (frozen or canned)
1 (15 oz) can black beans, drained and rinsed
1 (14.5 oz) can diced tomatoes * undrained
1 (8 oz) can tomato sauce
2 (4.5 oz) can green chiles, undrained
1 onion, chopped (about ½ cup)
3 cups chicken broth
3 chicken breasts, boneless skinless and cut in small pieces
1 package taco seasoning mix
Taco strips for garnishing*
Shredded cheddar cheese for garnishing
Sour cream for garnishing

In a crock pot mix corn, beans, diced tomatoes, tomato
    sauce, green chiles and onion.
Stir in broth, chicken and taco seasoning.
Cover and cook on Low for 8 hours or on High for 4 hours.
Garnishing with either tortillas stripes, cheese or sour cream.
Serves 6-8.

Tortillas—4 corn tortillas for garnishing--Instructions

Heat over at 425 degrees.
Brush each tortilla with oil.
Stack  tortillas, and cut into ¼ inch stripes.
Spread in single layer on a cookie sheet.
Sprinkle with salt and bake 7-10 minutes or until golden
    brown and crisp.
Garnish when soup is in the bowl.

Chicken Taco Soup© Connie Hope

# Connie's Cooking Tips

Some ideas to go 'Green" in your kitchen

- Cover a boiling pot.—It saves about one half the cooking time. It prevents heat loss and saves energy.

- Cooking for one—Try using a toaster oven. It will help save energy.

- Turn the heat off on the top of the stove or in the oven just before the time required to complete the recipe. The residual heat will finish cooking the item.

- Leftovers take less energy to reheat. Make extra and save in refrigerator or freeze for another meal.

- Grilling uses less energy and takes less time. It also keeps heat out of the house/kitchen. This can help reduce air conditioning costs.

- Use the right size burner on your stove. Don't put a small pot on a big burner. You just end up wasting the energy. You are heating the air around the pot.

- Buy fruits and 'veggies' locally. Support your local farmer's market.

- Buy organic food from your local farmer's market when you can. Important for your health. They don't use pesticides and are better for our environment.

- Instead of buying bottled water, get a filter pitcher or top filter. Many refrigerators have filtered water spouts built into them. So use it!

- Get out that old crock pot that Grandma used to use. Crock pots or slow cookers are low use of energy. You can make a great chili dish with one.

- Cleaning your stove top helps save energy. There is buildup on the electric stove coils that can reduce the amount of heat transmitted to a pot. Clean these coils more often. Also that vent at the bottom of your refrigerator needs to be cleaned for air circulation and energy efficiency. There are attachments to vacuum cleaners and brushes.

Removing fat from soup

1. Chill the soup. The fat rises to the top and will solidify when cold. Use a large spoon and skim to remove it.

2. Float a paper towel on the surface of the soup. It will absorb most of the fat.

Some thickening for soup:
• Barley
• Rice
• Noodles and dumplings
• Cut potatoes
• Mash potatoes
• 2-3 Tablespoons flour or cornstarch added to 1 cup water.

Make sure you stir continually in the same direction so that you don't get lumps.

Borsch is a soup made mostly of beets. It was a specialty in Eastern Europe and Russia.

# Soups and Stews with an International Flair

"I live on good soup, not on fine words"

**Moliere—French writer 1622-1673**

Soups are the greatest food to eat …and to make. You have it 'In addition… to the Entrée.' People say, "I am a master of soups." In fact, I have joked that it will go on my tombstone, 'She liked to make all kinds of soups made with all kinds of ingredients.'

Soups and stews can warm you when you are chilled or fill you if you are empty. There are hot soups, cold soups, and hot stews.

In this next section, I have put some of the International soups and stews favorites from friends around the world. Even my sister in law, who lives in Switzerland, has contributed a great recipe.

# Beet Soup or Borsch

(sometimes seen as Borscht)

There are as many variations of this soup as there are serving plates for soups. They can be served hot or cold. I prefer hot.

½ **cup carrot, chopped fine**
**1 cup onions, chopped fine**
**2 cups beets, cooked, chopped**
**2 cups beef stock—I like the stock in cans or boxes**
**1 cup very finely shredded cabbage**
**1 Tablespoon vinegar**
**Sour cream for topping**

Put all ingredients in a pot and cover with boiling water.
Simmer gently, covered, for 20 minutes, stirring often.
Add water if needed to cover and simmer 20 minutes more.
Place in serving bowl. Add 1 dollop of sour cream, serve with pumpernickel bread.
Serves 4-6.

# Borscht-variation

8 cups beef, chicken or vegetable broth
1 Tablespoon olive oil
2 onions, chopped
2-3 cloves of garlic, minced
1 teaspoon dried marjoram
2 celery stalks, sliced thin
2 parsnips, peeled, thinly sliced or chopped
1 carrot, peeled, thinly sliced
1 leek, white and light green parts, thinly sliced
½ head savory cabbage, shredded fine
1 bay leaf
Salt and pepper to taste
2 beets, peeled, and grated or chopped fine*
¼ cup dill, minced
3 Tablespoons red wine vinegar
½ cup sour cream for garnishing
1 Tablespoon horseradish (optional)

Bring the broth to a simmer while peeling the vegetables.
In a large soup pot, heat the oil.
Add onions and garlic, cook and stir until tender, 5 minutes.
Stir in the marjoram.
Add the celery, parsnips, carrot, leek and cabbage.
Cover and cook on low, stirring occasionally until vegetables
   are tender 8-10 minutes.
Add the bay leaf, salt, pepper and the broth, cook for about
   15 minutes.
Grate the beets directly into the soup.*
Simmer until vegetables are tender, about 15 minutes.
Stir in dill.
Add red wine vinegar, salt, pepper to taste.
Garnish soup with sour cream and/or horseradish.
Serves 6-8.

Borscht © Connie Hope

Borscht is a Ukrainian cabbage soup using root vegetables (beets, potatoes, onions, turnips, carrots) because they could be easily preserved in cool weather. Each Russian family cooked it in their own way, passing on the secret from generation to generation.
It can be served hot or cold.

*I prefer using fresh beets. I like their taste much better.

Cooking fresh beets-Clean outside of beets and cut off ends. Place in enough water to cover them. Boil for at least 10 minutes or until just starting to get soft. Save the juice to make pickled eggs. To remove skins, run beets under cold water and just put beet in your hands, gently pull down and the skin will pull right off.

Allow to cool, so you can grate them. Or you can finely chop them into the broth.

Irish Stew is a celebrated Irish dish, yet its composition is a matter of dispute.

Purists maintain that the only acceptable or traditional ingredients are mutton chops, potatoes, onions and water. Other would add carrots, turnips and pearl barley. I prefer the additional ingredients.

* Bouquet Garni is French for 'garnished bouquet' and is a bundle of herbs usually tied together with string. The classic recipe for Bonquet Garni is parsley, thyme and bay. Today, Rosemary, sage, and/or a stick of celery is added.

I prefer my stew a little thin with lots of broth. May need to add some broth.

Some people like it thick and add just a little instant mashed potatoes and stir until thickened. Your choice.

# Irish Stew--Traditional

2 medium onions, chopped
(1 cup chopped leeks can be added)
Olive oil for frying
1 ounce butter
1 sprig dried thyme
1 ½ pounds lamb cut in small pieces
7 carrots, chopped in 2 inch pieces
1 Tablespoon pearl barley
5 cups chicken stock-may need a little more
Salt and pepper to taste
1 Bouquet Garni *
12 medium potatoes, peeled
1 bunch parsley, leaves chopped finely
1 bunch chives

In a large pot, cook the onions in oil and butter over medium heat until they are translucent.
Add carrots and pearl barley.
In a separate pot, brown the lamb on high for a minute or two to seal in juices.
Pour the chicken stock so it covers the vegetables.
Add the meat.
Salt and pepper to taste.
Then add the Bouquet Garni.
Cover and cook on low for 2 hours. Do not boil.
Place potatoes on top of the stew and cover and cook for at least another 30 minutes until the potatoes are tender.
At this point the meat should be tender.
Serve in a large, flat soup bowl.
Add the parsley and chives as garnish and serve with crusty bread.
Serves 6-8.

Just the lamb browned for the Irish Stew © Connie Hope

# Favorite Irish Stew

1/3 cup flour, divided
1 ½ pounds lamb stew meat, cut into 1 inch cubes
3 Tablespoons olive oil, divided
3 medium onions, chopped. (I like sweet onions, Vidalia--
    if I can find them.)
3-4 garlic cloves, minced
4 cups beef both
2 medium potatoes, peeled and cubed
4 medium carrots, cut into 1 inch pieces
* (Optional: 2 parsnips or turnips cleaned and cut in cubes)
1 cup frozen peas
Salt and pepper to taste
1 teaspoon dried thyme
½ teaspoon Worcestershire sauce
2-3 Tablespoons water

Place 1/3 cup flour in a large re-sealable plastic bag.
Add lamb, a few pieces at a time, and shake to coat.
In a large soup pot, brown lamb in 2 Tablespoons oil.
Remove and set aside.
In the same pan, saute onions in remaining 1 Tablespoon oil.
Add garlic and cook 1-2 minutes.
Add broth, stirring to loosen browned bits from pan.
Return lamb to the pot.
Bring to a boil and reduce heat.
Cover and simmer for 1 hour or until meat is very tender.
Add potatoes and carrots. If desired, add parsnips or turnips*
Cover and cook for 20-30 more minutes.
Add seasonings and Worcestershire sauce.
Stir in peas and cook 5-10 minutes longer.
Combine small amount of flour in water, combine until
    smooth to thicken. Serve hot in a large bowl.
Serve with rolls or crusty bread.
Serves 6-8.

* You can also add 2 parsnips or turnips to the pot.

Variations:

1 Tablespoon fresh rosemary, leaves chopped

2 onions and one leek instead of the 3 onions.

Favorite Irish Stew © Connie Hope

*Regular oregano will do fine.

Mint leaves© Connie Hope

Variations:

½ pound of string beans, ends removed and cut into 1 inch pieces

A dash of cayenne

1 teaspoon dried oregano

# Albondigas Locas Soup

Albondigas means 'meatball' in Spanish. Some people call it 'Crazy Meatball Soup'. The trick to perfect Albondigas soup is the chopped mint leaves in the meatball. It's the mint that gives it a really interesting and unique flavor. This soup was originally introduced to the Spanish world from the Middle East during Islamic rule.

**For the meatballs:**
1 pound ground sirloin (or turkey)
1/3 cup rice, cooked
1 egg
2 cloves garlic, minced
¼ cup fresh mint leaves, chopped (2-3 teaspoons dried mint)
1/2 teaspoon dried Mexican oregano*
1/2 teaspoon cumin
Salt and pepper to taste

Preheat oven to 375 degrees.
Mix chopped meat and cooked rice.
Form into small meatballs and place on rack on baking
    sheet sprayed with non stick spray.
Bake until browned, 20-25 minutes. Turn at least once.
Set aside to cool.
Or microwave them for 5 plus minutes. Turn several times.
Or buy small meatballs at the supermarket. But you won't
    get the mint flavor if you buy them.

## Soup

2 teaspoon olive oil
1 onion, diced
2 carrots, diced
2 stalks celery, diced
2 cloves garlic, minced
8 cups chicken broth or a combination of chicken and beef
    broth (1 use Swanson reduced sodium)
1/2 cup long grain rice (or brown rice)
2-3 tomatoes, diced or 1 cup tomato puree or canned
    tomatoes (14.5 oz can)
1 teaspoon chili powder
1/2 tsp cumin
2 bay leaves
1/4 cup chopped cilantro leaves (fresh is best)

See next page

# (Albondigas Locas Soup continued)

1 zucchini, peeled, diced large
1 red bell pepper, diced
1 can corn-small
1 can peas-small
Salt and pepper to taste
Fresh limes
1 cup fresh cilantro, chopped

In a large stockpot, heat the oil.
Add the onion, carrots, celery, and saute until tender.
Add the garlic and stir about 30 seconds.
Add 8 cups of broth, tomatoes, chili powder, cumin, and
    bay leaves. Bring to a boil, stirring frequently.
Lower to simmer and add the zucchini and red pepper, peas
    and corn and cook for 1 hour.
Add the meatballs to the soup.  Simmer until the vegetables
    are tender, 20-30 minutes.
Serve with a squeeze of fresh lime and chopped cilantro as
    garnish.
Serves 6-8.

This soup is really tasty.  It's a little
more work, but worth it.

We had this soup on New Year's Eve 2011 at a friend's in Florida.
Thanks, Ginny,
I am sure we will stay warm with this great soup.

This recipe makes an enormous amount of soup.
There are three options: freeze some of it, cut the recipe in half or best of all invite lots of people to share in the fun.

Variations:
1-2 turnips, peeled and chopped

1-2 zucchini, peeled and chopped

1-2 large potatoes, peeled and diced

1 cup lentils, rinsed and drained

2 Tablespoons chopped cilantro

1 Tablespoon turmeric

1 cinnamon stick or 1
  teaspoon cinnamon

I also found a recipe that uses an immersion blender. Puree the soup until smooth. I personally like it chunky. Your choice. Experiment!

# Mulligatawny Soup

Mulligatawny means 'pepper water'. It is an English soup after an Indian recipe. It is based on an Indian dish (stew) that was changed into a soup for the fussy British soldiers when Britain ruled parts of South Asia and India from 1858 to 1947. It is believed to be loosely based on a stew the Brits loved that their Indian servants would often serve. It can have many different types of vegetables and sometimes no meats. The Brits added the chicken and called it a soup.

16 cups  chicken broth
6 lb chicken breasts, cooked, skinless, chopped
64 oz can tomatoes cut up, un-drained
4  cooking apples, peeled and chopped
3  onions, finely chopped
2 turnips, diced and skinned (optional)
6  carrots, chopped
6  celery stalks, chopped
2  green peppers, chopped
4 Tablespoons parsley, snipped just the ends
3 Tablespoons lemon juice
4 teaspoons sugar
4 teaspoons curry powder
1 teaspoon ground clove
8 cloves garlic, minced
Salt and pepper to taste

In a large soup pot, combine broth, cooked chicken,
    un-drained tomatoes, apples, onions, carrots, celery,
     turnips (optional) peppers, parsley, lemon juice, sugar,
      curry powder, ground cloves, garlic, salt and pepper.
Bring to boiling; reduce heat.
Cover; simmer for 20-30 minutes, stirring occasionally.
Serves 8-10 or a gang.

Mulligatawny Soup© Connie Hope

# Polish Meatball Cabbage Soup

2 heads cabbage-cut in quarters, then each sliced thin
6   14 oz cans diced tomato or tomato sauce
1 large onion, chopped
3 Tablespoons lemon juice (fresh is best)
3 Tablespoons sugar
1 Fresh tomato, cut in quarters
2 beef cubes in 1 cup boiling water
Mix for meatballs (see below)

To make meat balls:
2 pounds fat free ground meat (or turkey ground meat)
3 eggs
1 cup bread crumbs
½ cup cooked rice

Combine meat ball ingredients and roll into meat balls.
I put them in the microwave and heat a little to make sure most
  of the fat is removed.  Place on a paper towel.
    (You can also use pre-made meatballs or bake in the oven).

For Soup:

Combine all ingredients except meat balls.
Cook slowly for several hours.
Add meat balls and cook for 1 hour more.
Serves 8-10 or more.

Polish Meatball Cabbage Soup© Connie Hope

This is a great soup when it is chilly outside and you need something to warm you.  It makes a large amount of soup.
I have cut the recipe in half and it works well.

This is from my first cookbook, *In Addition ...to the Entrée.*

* I prefer the acini di pepe, which are the small balls of pasta. Great in many dishes.  They are sometimes difficult to find.  Most Italian markets or Italian delicatessens should have them.

Two methods to cook the meatballs:

1. Heat oven at 350 degrees, place meatballs on a cookie sheet, and bake for 30 minutes or until cooked.  Set aside.

2. Or you can microwave them and turn them 2 times.  Start with 2 minutes, turn them for another 2 minutes.
Check for doneness and, if more time is needed, add another 2 minutes.

(continued on next page)

# Italian Wedding Soup (also called Chicken Escarole Soup)

12-18 meatballs—smaller than the normal meatball size and fully cooked
1 Tablespoon olive oil
1 medium onion, minced
2-3 carrots, diced
2 stalks celery
1-2 cloves garlic, minced
¼ cup white wine (optional)
8 cups chicken broth
1/4 cup small pasta (stars, ditalini or acini di pepe) *
1 teaspoon basil, dried
12 oz baby spinach  or Escarole, washed and trimmed
Salt and pepper to taste
¼ cup fresh parsley, chopped
¼ cup Parmesan cheese for topping

## Meatballs

There are two options for the meatballs. You can purchase pre-cooked meatballs, but be choosy about the size. These should be smaller than the normal meatball.  Or make them yourself. Here's the recipe:
1 pound ground beef or turkey
1 egg
¼ cup bread crumbs
1 small clove garlic, minced
Salt and pepper to taste
1 Tablespoon fresh parsley, finely chopped (or 1 teaspoon dried)
2 Tablespoons Parmesan cheese

Mix all ingredients in a large bowl and form small meatballs.  If I have extra meatballs, I cook them all and then freeze the extra for next time.
Cook meatballs (see two methods for cooking meatballs)

Italian Wedding Soup © Connie Hope

# Italian Wedding Soup (continued)

In a large soup pot, saute onion, carrots, and celery over
   medium heat until tender.
Add garlic and basil and stir for 2-4 minutes medium heat.
Salt and pepper to taste.
Add broth and wine (optional) and bring to a boil.
Add pasta and spinach and carefully put in the meatballs.
Simmer for about 25 minutes.
Stir in parsley and top with Parmesan cheese.
Serves 6-8.

Two types of small pasta– ditalini or
acini di pepe.

Onions  ©  Connie Hope

A nice crusty bread is great with
this. Makes me hungry just thinking
about it.

Italian Wedding Soup © Connie Hope

I will also put this in the crock pot/ slow cooker section. 4 hours on High or 8 hours on Low. Stir in the fish during the last hour of cooking.

Jambalaya © Connie Hope

*File powder is a necessity for cooking authentic Creole or Cajun cuisine. Gumbo file powder is the powdered leaves of the sassafras tree.

Emeril's Essence Creole Seasoning (known as Bayou Blast):
1 ½ T paprika
2 T salt
2 T garlic powder
1 T pepper
1 T cayenne pepper
1 T dried oregano
1 T dried thyme

Combine all ingredients

# Jambalaya

Jambalaya is a popular Louisiana Creole dish of Spanish and French influence. It has been a favorite dish for generations because it is inexpensive, delicious and can be altered with many different meats and seafood. Traditionally, the meat included sausage of some sort and can have other meats (ham, duck, turtle or boar (Ha) or seafood (crawfish, oysters, shrimp and others). The vegetables are a mixture known as the 'Holy Trinity' in Creole and Cajun cooking. It consists of onions, celery and green bell peppers—although other vegetables such as carrots, tomatoes, chilies and garlic are also used. A basic recipe for Jambalaya: 'When your rice is done, your Jambalaya is done.'

**2 Tablespoons oil, divided**
**1 Tablespoon Cajun seasoning**
**10 oz sausage, sliced in rounds**
**1 pound chicken breasts, skinless, cut in 1 inch pieces**
**1 onion, diced**
**1 medium green pepper, diced**
**2-3 stalks of celery, diced**
**3-4 cloves of garlic, minced**
**1 can (16 oz) diced or crushed Italian tomatoes**
**½ teaspoon red pepper flakes**
**Salt and pepper to taste**
**½ teaspoon hot pepper sauce**
**2 teaspoons Worcestershire sauce**
**1 teaspoon file powder***
**1 ¼ cups uncooked white rice**
**2 ½ cups chicken broth**

Heat 1 Tablespoon oil in a large soup pot over medium heat.
Season the sausage and chicken with Cajun Seasoning.
Saute sausage until browned.
Remove with a slotted spoon, set aside to drain.
Add 1 Tablespoon oil and saute chicken pieces until lightly browned on all sides.
Remove with a slotted spoon and set aside. Drain.
In the same pot, saute onion, bell pepper, celery and garlic until tender.
Stir in crushed (or diced) tomatoes and season with red pepper, salt and pepper, hot pepper sauce, Worcestershire sauce and file powder.
Stir in chicken and sausage.
Cook on simmer for 20-30 minutes. Stirring occasionally.
Stir in rice and chicken broth and bring to a boil, reduce heat, simmer another 30 minutes or until the liquid is absorbed and rice is done.
Serves 4-6.

# Pasta e Fagioli (pasta and beans)

Ham bone
Several slices of ham, chopped
3 Tablespoons of olive oil
1 ½ cups celery
1 cup onions, minced
1 bag (1 pound) Great Northern beans
3-4 cloves of garlic
½ teaspoon dried basil, dried oregano
2 Tablespoons chopped parsley
Salt and pepper to taste
4 cups chicken broth
Pasta (about two cups cooked, but more is better)
1  26 oz jar of spaghetti sauce, use your homemade or use
     chopped or stewed tomatoes

Follow the instruction on the beans and soak 1 pound of
    beans overnight in 6-8 cups of water.
Rinse beans and drain before using.
Put olive oil in a large soup pot.
Add the celery, onions and garlic sauté at low heat. Stir.
When almost cooked, add the chopped ham.
Add the chicken broth, the ham bone and the beans.
Bring to a boil and turn down to low for 3 hours.
Cook pasta separately, add to soup.
Add spaghetti sauce (or stewed or chopped tomatoes).
Reheat to serve.
Serve with crusty bread.
Serves 6-8.

You can easily double this recipe.

At Christmas and other holidays, I usually bake a ham. I always put the ham bone in a plastic bag and stick it in the freezer for future cooking.

The pasta for this soup is your choice. There are so many great ones. I also use leftover pasta if I have it. Bow ties (farfalle), small or medium shells, ditali, anelli (small rings), macaroni, penne, or spaghetti broken into thirds.

This was given to me by a friend many years ago. Maryanne was Italian and loved to cook soup. Thanks for the recipe. It is one of my most used. I miss you.

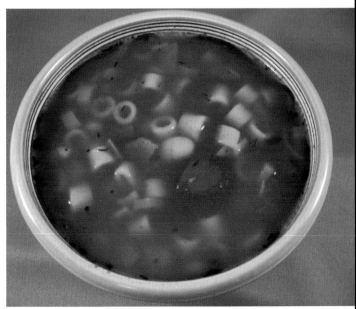

©Connie Hope  Pasta e Fagioli

* Try using 'Better than Bouillon'. See Appendix

** At the supermarket, you can now buy a package of linguine or spaghetti that is already cut in half. Go figure.

Variation:

You can add a can (15 oz) garbanzo beans or navy beans, drained and rinsed.

Also substitute the crushed tomatoes for diced tomatoes. It makes it a different consistency.

2 cups of green beans, cut.
(I love the beans in the soup)

1 cup chopped fennel bulb

# Italian Sausage Soup

5-6 Italian sausages, sliced
1 large onion, sliced
6 cups water (or use beef broth)*
1 can (28 oz) tomatoes, crushed, undrained
2 zucchini, small quartered and sliced
½ cup green pepper, chopped
1 Tablespoon beef bouillon*
½ teaspoon dried basil
½ teaspoon dried oregano
Salt and pepper to taste
3 oz uncooked linguine, broken in two**
3 Tablespoons Parmesan cheese-grated is best

In a large soup pot, cook sausage and onion over medium
    heat until sausage is cooked inside.
Stir in water (or broth), tomatoes, zucchini, green pepper,
    bouillon, basil, oregano, salt and pepper.
Bring to a boil, stir in linguine, and cover and simmer for 15-
    20 minutes or until the linguine is tender.
Serve in a bowl with a sprinkle of cheese on top.
Serves 8.

Italian Sausage Soup © Connie Hope

# Italian Vegetable Soup

5 cups mixed chopped vegetables*
3 cups Pinto beans (you can use Borlotti beans, which you can get at the Italian market, rinsed and drained.)
2-3 cloves garlic, minced
2 Tablespoons olive oil
I teaspoon oregano
I teaspoon basil
Salt and pepper to taste
2 Tablespoons fresh parsley, chopped
¾ cup tomato puree
7-8 cups vegetable broth
Pinch of pepper flakes
I ¼ cups small pasta

In a soup pot, put oil and garlic, vegetables, beans, spices, tomato puree, broth.
Stir and bring to a boil, simmer for 35-45 minutes.
Salt and pepper to taste.
Add pasta and cook until tender.
Serves 5-6.

# Chinese Clam Chowder

2 Tablespoons lemongrass in the tube*
I teaspoon butter
2 cups baking potatoes, peeled and cut in ½ cubes
I cup onion, chopped
I cup celery, chopped
I Tablespoon fresh ginger, peeled and grated or minced
2 -3 cloves garlic, minced
I ½ Tablespoons fish sauce
2 (8 oz) bottles of clam juice
¾ cup zucchini, peeled and chopped
2 ( 6 ½ oz) cans clams, chopped and drained
I Serrano chili, seeds removed and veins, thinly sliced **
2/3 cup light coconut milk
¼ cup lime juice (fresh is best)
Salt and pepper
2 Tablespoons fresh cilantro, chopped

Put butter in a soup pot, add potatoes, onions, celery, ginger, garlic, salt and pepper to taste .
Cook until tender, 5-8 minutes.
Stir in lemongrass, fish sauce, and clam juice.
Boil, then reduce to simmer for 10-15 minutes.
When potatoes are tender, stir in zucchini, clams and chili.
Bring to a boil, simmer for 5 minutes until zucchini is tender.
Stir in coconut milk, lime juice and cilantro.
Serves 4-6.

*Here are some of the ones that I use, but experiment.

Kale
Cabbage
Carrots
Celery
Broccoli
Zucchini
Spinach
Japanese eggplant

*You can also use 2 Tablespoons lemongrass powder.

** If you like things spicy, increase the Serrano pepper to 2, but it does make it spicy. Removing the seeds and veins makes it milder.

Fennel

Sautéed fennel and onion.

# Italian Chicken Soup with Fennel

1 fennel bulb, chopped in small pieces
1 medium onion, chopped
2 teaspoons olive oil
2 cups hot water
4 cups chicken broth
1 ½ cups carrots, chopped
Salt and pepper to taste
¼ teaspoon dried thyme
¼ teaspoon dried basil
2 cups chicken breast, cubed and cooked
½ cup uncooked orzo pasta
2 Tablespoons fennel fronds, chopped fine

In a soup pot, saute fennel bulb and onion in oil until tender.
Add water, chicken broth, carrots, salt, pepper thyme, and basil.
Bring to a boil, reduce heat. Cover and simmer for 20 minutes.
Stir in chicken and orzo.
Cover and cook 20 minutes, until orzo is tender.
Stir in fennel fronds for garnish.
Serves 4.

Italian Chicken Soup with Fennel © Connie Hope

# History of Vichyssoise.

Vichyssoise, which has been enjoyed for decades, is a chilled potato and leek soup  Its creation has been credited to a French Chef, Louis Diate at the New York Ritz-Carlton Hotel in 1917. He called it Crème Vichyssoise Glacier or chilled Cream Vichyssoise. He named it for the town of Vichy, France where he was born. This basic recipe was given to Diate by his mother and to which he added some cream to her recipe and served it cold with chopped chive on the top.

There is some controversy around this story.  Jules Gouffe's Royal Cookery Book (1869) contained a recipe for potato and leek soup. The only difference was that Gouffe's soup was hot and Diate's was served cold.   1

There is also a second story that King Louis XV of France accidently invented vichyssoise. The King loved his comforting potato soup and had it for dinner often. He was always nervous that someone was trying to poison him, so the King demanded that several servants taste his food before he ate it.  Several servants would taste the soup and by the time it got back to the King, it was cold.  King Louis decided he preferred his potato-leek soup cold.  And this is how the French came to eat their vichyssoise cold.     2

Here is French Chef, Louis Diat's recipe from 1941:

**4 leeks, white part**
**1 medium onion**
**2 oz sweet butter**
**5 medium potatoes**
**1 quart water or chicken broth**
**1 Tablespoon salt**
**2 cups milk**
**2 cups medium cream**
**1 cup heavy cream**

Finely slice the white part of the leek and the onion and brown very lightly in sweet butter, add the potatoes, also sliced thin. Add water or broth and salt.  Boil slowly for 25-30 minutes.  Crush and rub through a fine strainer.* Return heat, add 2 cups cream. Season and bring to a boil. Cool and then rub through a very fine strainer.  When soup is cold, add heavy cream.  Chill before serving.  Finely chopped chives as garnish."   3
Serves 4-5.

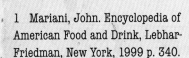

1   Mariani, John. Encyclopedia of American Food and Drink, Lebhar-Friedman, New York, 1999 p. 340.

2  Chris Albano, article October 10, 2008: Vichyssoise, History & Beyond, found on www.suite101.com

3 Louis Diat, Cooking A La Ritz, J.B. Lippincott: New York, 1941, p. 68

* Today, we can use an immersion blender to puree the mixture.

It isn't always possible to find the fresh herb in a recipe, or the dried herb when you need it. The rule of thumb for most herbs is:

1 teaspoon of the dried herb
= 1 tablespoon of the fresh

Vegan Vichyssoise:

Substitute:
vegan margarine for the
    butter.
5 cups of vegetable broth
Use ½ cup soy milk and
    add 1-2 Tablespoons
    cornstarch.
Heat soy milk and add cornstarch
with wire whisk.
Allow to cool and add to soup.

If you like your soup really creamy, you can change it. Use 4 cups of broth and 1 ½ cups heavy cream. Add a dash of nutmeg. Take out the thyme and marjoram and bay leaf and try it without.

# Vichyssoise Soup Cold

1 Tablespoon butter
5 leeks, cut into rings use some of the green
1 onion, chopped
5 Russet potatoes, peeled and sliced thin
Salt and pepper to taste
¼ teaspoon dried thyme (1/2 teaspoon fresh thyme)
½ teaspoon dried marjoram( 1 teaspoon fresh marjoram)
1 bay leaf
5 cups chicken broth (can substitute vegetable broth)
½ cup heavy whipping cream

In a soup pot, melt butter over low heat.
Add leeks and onion and stir.
Cook about 10 minutes or until they are translucent.
Add potatoes and seasonings.
Stir and then cover to cook for about 10-15 minutes
Remove bay leaf.
Put mixture in a food processor or immersion blender and
    puree.  Chill soup
When ready to serve, add the cream.
This can also be served hot. Be careful after adding cream
    when heating as to not change the consistency.
Serves 5-6.

Variation for Vichyssoise :

Here are two variations, but I am sure you can think of many more.
Experiment.

1. Carrot Vichyssoise

    Use the standard Vichyssoise recipes and add 5 carrots, peeled and sliced.
    Add to mix and food process and blend until smooth.

2. Zucchini vichyssoise

    Add 3 cups zucchini, chopped and add to mix.
    Use the  food processor or immersion blender and blend until smooth.
    Garnish with chives and pieces of cut zucchini.

    Add a dash  of nutmeg
    Take out the thyme and marjoram and bay leaf and try it without it.
    Add chive for garnishing.

# Thai Hot and Sour Soup

6 cups chicken broth (can use vegetable broth)
4 dried shitake mushrooms*
6 dried wood ear mushrooms*
3 cups warm water
1 can (6 oz) bamboo shoots, cut into slices
1 inch piece of ginger, peeled and finely chopped
1 (5 oz) block of firm, silken Tofu cut in to 1./2 inc cubes
2 teaspoons soy sauce
2 Tablespoons rice wine or use red wine
5 Tablespoons cornstarch, mixed in ¼ cup water
2-3 Tablespoons red vinegar
Chopped cilantro or green onion for garnish

Put broth in a soup pot and set aside.
Place dried mushrooms in a small bowl and cover with 3 cups warm water.
Set aside 15-20 minutes until mushrooms absorb the water.
Strain mushroom infused liquid into the pot with broth.**
Remove touch center of wood ear mushroom and discard.
Cut mushroom into slivers and set aside.
Bring liquid to a boil, then reduce and simmer adding
    mushrooms, ginger and bamboo for 5-7 minutes.
Add tofu and simmer until tofu is warm about 4-5 minutes.
Add soy sauce and wine and stir.
Whisk in cornstarch a little at a time to thicken.
Turn off heat and add vinegar, salt and pepper to taste.
Garnish with cilantro or green onions.
Serves 4-5.

# Egg Drop Soup

4 cups chicken broth
4 oz Chinese ham, Chinese dried sausage or slab of bacon
6 scallions, greens thinly sliced
1 inch ginger, peeled and grated
Salt and peppercorns to taste
4 teaspoons cornstarch
2 whole eggs

Combine stock, ham, scallion, ginger, salt, pepper in a pot.
Bring to a boil, then simmer for 30-40 minutes.
Strain broth, discard solids.
Combine 1 Tablespoon cornstarch and 1 Tablespoon water
    in a small bowl, mix with fork.
Whisk into broth and bring to a simmer.
Whisk together eggs and remaining cornstarch.
Transfer eggs to a small bowl and slowly drizzle egg mixture
    into soup. Sit for 1 minute. Stir gently to break up eggs
    with a fork. Sprinkle with scallions.
Serves 4.

*Can be found in Asian Markets. If you can't find them, use fresh shitake and/or button mushrooms

Variation: You can add a pound of shrimp, cooked and peeled to the soup. Or chicken breast, chopped.

** If you have used fresh mushrooms, take 3 cups of warm water and put 'Better than Bouillon' Mushroom base in it. It will make it really tasty. Just put this mix into the pot.

The trick is slowly drizzle egg mixture and use a fork to break up eggs.

My sister-in-law lives in Switzerland and uses this pot of stew recipe often. It is a French pot of stew. You can feed a family of 4 for several days. Thanks, Anne and Mom Hope

Bouquet garni is a bundle of herbs usually tied together with string and used in soups and stew. It is removed before serving. You can include any of the following:

- 4 parsley sprigs
- 4 thyme sprigs
- 2 bay leaves
- Basil
- Chervil
- Rosemary
- Tarragon
- savory

## Bon Appetit!

# Mom Hope's Pot au Feu*

1 to 1 ½ pound of beef for stewing
Beef marrow bones
Beef short ribs
8 medium potatoes, peeled and cut in chunks
6-8 carrots, cut in small rounds
6 leeks, finely sliced
2 large onions
6 stalks celery, chopped small
4 cups water
3-4 beef bouillon cubes
Provincial herbs or Bouquet garni*
Salt and pepper to taste
Serve with crusty bread
Horseradish (optional)

Additional can be added:
6 medium parsnips, peeled and cut in 2 inch length
6 medium turnips, peeled and quartered
1 pound rutabagas, peeled and cut into eighths

In a soup pot, add 4 cups water, bouillon cubes, bones and herbs.
Add beef, carrots, onions, leeks, garlic, and celery. Add any
   additional vegetables that you might like.
Simmer for 2 hours. Stir occasionally.
Cook the potatoes separately, then add to pot in last 30
   minutes.
Remove the Bouquet garni before serving.
Invite the neighbors and friends, as this is a great sharing meal.
Serve with French crusty bread. Horseradish is optional.
Serves 6-8 or more.

Pot au Feu© Connie Hope

# Moroccan Chicken Stew

1 chicken, cut in small serving pieces
1 cup onions chopped
6 cloves of garlic, minced
½ cup fresh parsley, chopped
1/3 cup fresh mint, chopped
1 teaspoon ground cardamom
1 teaspoon cumin
¼ teaspoon ground saffron
¼ cup olive oil
¼ cup lemon juice
1 ½ cups chicken broth
2 cinnamon sticks
Peel of 1 orange
1 (14.5 oz) can chick peas
½ cup pitted prunes
½ cup pitted olives
1 large can plum tomatoes

Place chicken in large bowl.
Combine with next 8 ingredients(onion to lemon juice).
Marinate chicken for up to 8 hours (overnight).
Place in large pot with broth, cinnamon sticks and orange
    peel. Salt and pepper to taste.
Bring to a boil, reduce and simmer for 30 minutes.
Add chickpeas, prunes, olives and tomatoes and simmer for
    30 minutes.
Remove cinnamon sticks and peels.
Serve over couscous or pasta.
Serves 5-6.

This is from Mary Pusissegur.

Many years ago she returned from Istanbul with an abundance of exotic spices from the Spice Bazaar. She asked a friend on Food Network what to do with all the spices. Here is the recipe he gave to her.

Variations that I found:
½ cup raisins instead of
    prunes
2 cups green peas
¼ cup slivered almonds for garnish.

Moroccan Chicken Stew © Connie Hope

This is from my friend, Mary Puissegur. Maw-Maw was her maternal grandmother. The recipe is over 100 years old. The Landry's were sugar cane farmers down-river from New Orleans. When the family got together, they would serve this gumbo along with seafood boil of blue crab, crawfish and shrimp. You will love it!

*You can also use 'Better than Bouillon' either fish or chicken.

*The Roux-two ways:

First:
¾ cup flour
¾ cup butter
Melt in heavy bottomed skillet. Slowly sprinkle in flour a little at a time. Stir constantly. Watch it for 30 minutes. Do Not Burn.

Second:
1 cup vegetable oil
1 cup flour
Heat oil until hot.
Gradually add flour, stirring constantly.
Reduce and cook for 30 minutes, stir constantly.
Do Not Burn.

# Maw-Maw Landry's Gumbo

1 ½  pounds cleaned shrimp
6 live blue crabs or 2 cans crabmeat
¼ pound andouille or smoked sausage
2 pounds fresh or frozen okra, chopped
3 onions, chopped
3 cloves garlic, minced
½ green pepper, chopped
4-6 cups water (*or use fish or chicken stock*)*
1 can stewed tomatoes-large
1 Tablespoon cooking oil
2 bay leaves
½ teaspoon thyme
3 sprigs parsley
2 dashes cayenne
1 teaspoon gumbo file
Salt and pepper to taste
Dash of liquid crab boil, optional
The Roux * (*a thickener used as a base in many Creole dishes*)
3 Tablespoons flour
3 Tablespoons oil

In a large pot with 1 T oil, lightly brown the onions, pepper and garlic.
Add okra and ½ cup liquid, simmer 45 minutes.
In a separate skillet, add oil and flour to make the Roux.
Brown on medium heat, stirring constantly, until the Roux is the color of peanut butter.
Add the Roux to the vegetables, add tomatoes and spices.
Add remaining liquid, one cup at a time while stirring.
Add sausage. Cover and simmer 1-2 hours. Add more liquid if needed.
30 minutes before serving, add shrimp and crab.
Serve over rice.
Serves 8-10.

Maw-Maw Landry's Gumbo © Connie Hope

# Connie's Cooking Tips

**Microwave use—**
• **What effects the cooking time?**
**1. Density of the moisture in the food**
**2. The weight of the food**
**3. The wattage of the microwave**
**4. The temperature of the food at time you start microwaving**
**5. The shape or form of the food.**

• Why reducing moisture when cooking in a microwave?
The microwave cooks things much more quickly. You need to reduce the moisture in conventional recipes by about one fourth. Here is an example. If your recipe calls for a cup of liquid (ie. water, broth, etc.), reduce it to three quarters of a cup.

• Herbs in a recipe that you are going to microwave--
If you are using an oven recipe, use less of the spice than it calls for. Their flavors do not evaporate in a microwave as they do in an oven.

• One cup of water boils in two and half minutes. The average food takes about one forth the time required in a conventional oven. For example, if your recipe takes on hour to cook in an oven, it should take about fifteen minutes in a microwave. Nothing is written in stone. The name of the game is experiment.

• Check recipe times that are for the microwave in comparison to a oven recipe. There is not an accurate science, but the rule of thumb is approximately one-forth of the oven time is needed for a microwave recipe. Practice or try is the rule. Fish, chicken and meats; be very careful with the time. Remember the items density does affect the time. When in doubt, check it out. Check another recipe that is similar for the time.

Removing outside skin of garlic with ease.
Put several cloves of garlic on a paper towel in the microwave. Set the timer for 15 seconds or less. The outside skin will peel away with ease. Give it a few minutes to cool down.

• Removing outside skin of garlic with ease: Put several cloves of garlic on a moist paper towel in the microwave. Set the timer for 15 to 20 seconds. The outside skin will peel away with ease. Give it a few minutes to cool down.

# APPENDIX

Recipes exist to get

ideas from, not

necessarily to follow

exactly.

## Experiment!

# APPENDIX
# Herbs and Spices

Storing

The difference between an herb and a spice is a fine line. The main difference is knowing where the plant came from and which part of the plant is used. Spices tend to come from plants grown in a more tropical climate. Herbs can grow in many climates and sometime even in the home. The other difference is how the herb or spices is used in cooking. Herbs are used in larger portion in flavoring foods. Species are usually stronger in taste and used in smaller amounts. Condiments such as prepared mustard, catsup, Worcestershire, Tabasco sauce, and other steak sauce are a combination of herbs and spices blended in a liquid form.

Herbs are leaves of plants that are very aromatic. They can be used fresh or dried. Examples are parsley, rosemary, dill, oregano, basil, chives, marjoram, thyme and many others.

**Spices come from the bark, roots, buds, seeds, berry or fruit of tropical trees and plants.**
   **Bark—cinnamon**
   **Root ginger, onion, garlic**
   **Buds—cloves, saffron**
   **Seeds-yellow mustard, poppy, sesame, cumin, and**
        **nutmeg**
   **Berry-black pepper**
   **Fruit—allspice, paprika**

Dried herbs can lose potency as they age. You may need to add a little more to obtain the flavor you like. Taste what you are making often and add alter accordingly to your own taste. It is always better to use a light hand and add as you need it. Taking away flavor is not an option.

Fresh herbs can be put in a paper towel and stored in a re-sealable plastic bag and then put into the refrigerator or even the freezer. Dried herbs should be stored out of the light and in a dry, cool place. They should be stored in a glass or plastic container with a tight lid. They are stored away from moisture. Dampness can cause loss of taste. The whole spices or herbs last longer than ones that are already ground. Herbs and spices can be crusted with a mortar and piston or by using a rolling pin between a towel. You can also store in the refrigerator or freezer.
Always taste the mix after it has heated for a little while.

extending cooking time such as in a crock pots may take away from the herbs intensity, so keep tasting the mix.

Different parts of the world have their own food tastes and use different herbs and spices to obtain this. Tasting food from various cultures gives us an idea what different herbs and spices add to their food. Oregano and basil are connected to Italian food. Curries are used in Indian food. Today supermarkets have a great variety of herbs and spices. It makes it easy to try and experiment with them.

Many people have asked me to write a little about some of the herbs and spices, their flavors, and what they are used with. I have put together a short list with pictures of some.

### Allspice-spice(ground)

Dark brown pea-size berries form the evergreen pimento tree, which is in the myrtle family. The berry is dried and its about the size of a peppercorn. It can be used in anything from salads to desserts--in pickling spice, spiced tea mixes, cakes as well as in ketchup, pickles and sausages. The flavor is a pungent, sweet mixture similar to the tastes of cinnamon, clove and nutmeg.

### Anise Seed-spice (whole or ground)

Small green-brown seed. It is a member of the parsley family. The taste is a sweet licorice flavor. It is used in breads, cakes, candies, cookies, fruit and some Italian sausages.

### Basil-herb( fresh leaves or dried and crumbled)

It is a member of the mint family. Most varieties have a green leaf, sometimes a purple color. It has a sweet, peppery, clove-like flavor that is pungent and aromatic. It is wonderful cut fresh from a garden. There are many uses for basil in cooking—chicken, eggs, fish, pasta, pesto, tomatoes. It is used in many Italian and Mediterranean recipes.

### Bay Leaf-herb (dried whole leaves, )

Bay leafs are from the evergreen bay laurel tree (which is also known as laurel leaf or bay laurel). It has a pungent, earthy aroma and best used dried. These leaves can be used in soups, stews, tomato sauces, sauces for meats and vegetables.

### Caraway seed-spice

(dried whole seeds) These seeds have a sweet nutty flavor, also licorice flavor, and are best when used whole. They are herbs in the parsley family best known for use on rye bread. It can be used on sauerkraut, noodles, cheese spreads, breads, pickling, vegetables, cookies, herbal vinegars and found with German, Austrian, and some Hungarian recipes. One of my favorite uses is on sauerkraut and pork.

**Cardamom-spice** (whole pod, seeds or ground) Seeds are in pods and about the size of a cranberry. They are a member of the ginger family. The flavor is spicy-sweet, pungent aroma. It comes from India, Guatemala, and Ceylon. It is used in curry and stews, some cookies, cakes and breads.

**Cayenne Pepper-spice** (ground) A hot spice best used dried ground, fresh finely chopped. Use this in food you want to have hot and spicy. Powdered seasoning is made from a variety of tropical chilies, including red cayenne pepper. It is also called Red Pepper. It is dark red in color and looks like paprika. The flavor is said to be hot and pungent. It is used on eggs, cheese, most Cajun recipes. History has it that it was also used to help with the pain related to stomachaches and gas, to improve and treat diseases of the circulatory system, and as a treatment for arthritic and rheumatic pain. It is named after the city Cayenne in French Guyana. And it is also used to make mace or pepper spray.

**Celery Seed-spice** (whole or ground or mixed with salts to be celery salts) It is the seed from wild Indian celery called lovage. It has a very strong celery flavor, but can be slightly bitter. It is used in sauces, soups, stews, salads (potato or cole slaw) and stuffing.

**Chervil-herb** (fresh springs or crumbled dried) It has curly, dark green leaves and is in the parsley family. It has a mild celery-anise flavor. It is used in eggs, chicken, fish shellfish and salads.

**Chili powder-spice** (ground) Seasoning blend made from ground dried chilies, coriander, cumin, garlic, oregano and other herbs and spices. Mild to hot in flavor. It is used in chili, eggs, soups, stews and man Mexican dishes.

**Chives-herb** (fresh stalks, or dried) It is a slender green grass like with a hollow stems. It is related to the onion or leek and has a mild onion taste. It is snipped and used for garnishing. It is used on appetizers, soups, fish, salads, eggs and many cheese dishes.

**Cilantro-herb** (fresh or dried chopped leaves) It comes from the coriander plant and resembles parsley. In American cooking, the fruits (or seeds) are generally referred to as coriander, the leaves as cilantro. It is also called Chinese parsley. There is a big taste difference between the leaves and seeds. The leaves have a very pungent smell and taste and are used to season many foods. The seeds have a spicy, lemony taste and aroma. Cilantro is used with fish, rice, salsas, salads and Italian, Latin American, and Mexican recipes.

**Cinnamon-spice** (whole stick or ground) It is the inner bark from a Ceylon or Cassia tree which has a dark reddish to brown bark. It is aromatic and pungent. The sticks are added during the cooking process for flavor and are not meant to be eaten. Cinnamon is used in cakes, cookies, hot drinks, pies, vegetables such as carrots winter squash, sweet potatoes and Brussels sprouts. My favorite use is in my coffee in the morning. It is reported to aid in lowering your cholesterol and assist in stabilizing diabetes.

**Clove-spice** (whole or ground) It comes from the Latin word that means nail. The clove is reddish brown and looks similar to a small nail. It comes from buds from the tropical evergreen clove tree. It is aromatic, pungent and sweet. The flavor can be overpowering, so use with care. It is used in baked beans, soups, stews, fruit pies, ham pickling, spice cakes and cookies. I like to use clove to dot the sides and top of a baked ham. It adds such a great flavor.

**Coriander-spice** (whole or ground) Coriander is the seeds from the coriander plant, which is in the parsley family (see cilantro). The flavor is a combination of lemon, sage and caraway. It is used in baking, pickling, soups, stews, meats and marinades. It is used in Mexican and Spanish recipes. It is said to that coriander was the first spice to arrive in American

**Cumin-spice** (whole or ground) Cumin is a dried fruit from a plant in the parsley family. Slightly bitter with a smoky, nutty, hot flavor. It is used in chilies and curry blends, beans, chicken, eggplant, fish, lamb, lentils, sausage. The ingredients are used in Middle Eastern, Asian, Mediterranean, and Mexican cuisines.

**Dill Seed-spice** (whole or ground) Dried seed from the dill plant, Tangy, 'dill pickle' flavor, more pungent than the herb. It is used in meats, chickens, salads, sauces, and many vegetables.

**Dill Weed-herb** (fresh whole or dried) Feathery green leaves from the dill plant. It is pungent, tangy flavoring. It is used in breads, fish, pickling, salads, sauces, and vegetables. Dill is the predominant seasoning in pickling recipes. It is also added to flavor sauerkraut and potato salad.

**Fennel Seeds-spices** (dried whole) It is oval, greenish-brown seed from the fennel plant. It is aromatic, slight licorice flavored and larger than anise seed. It is used in breads, fish, chicken, sauces, sausage, soups, stews and many Italian recipes.

**Ginger-spice (fresh, dried, crystallized or ground)** It is a gnarled and bumpy root from the ginger plant. It has a slightly peppery, and sweet taste with a pungent and spicy aroma. The mature root is fibrous and nearly dry. It is used in many salsas, breads, cakes, cookies (such as gingerbread) and Asian dishes. It can be pickled and sliced thin and served with sushi. For storage, the ginger should be wrapped in a towel, placed in a plastic bag, and kept in the refrigerator or freezer.

**Juniper Berries-spice (dried whole)** Slightly soft berries that resemble the size and color of a blue berry. They are pungent, piney flavor, bitter when raw, principle flavoring in the alcoholic beverage, gin. It is used in sauerkraut, marinades, and as a curing mix for salmon.

**Lavender-herb** Lavender has been documented in use for over 2,500 years. In ancient times lavender was used for mummification and perfume. The lavender plant was introduced to America around 1600's. Cooking with lavender is fun, but experimental. Start out with a small amount and add more as you go. Motto—a little goes a long way. Use it in breads, salads, roasts, stews, soups and even coffee and tea. There is nothing better than lavender tea! This is one of my favorite herbs to use in cooking.

**Lemon Grass-herb (fresh or dried stalks or ground)** Long, think gray-green leaves. It has a lemony flavor and fragrance and is very fibrous. Lemon grass is used with fish, chicken, shellfish, soups and stews. It is used in Thai and Indonesian recipes.

**Mace-spice (dried blades or ground)** Mace and nutmeg are similar, but mace is more powerful. It is bright red outer covering (the nutmeg seed) and will turn yellow-orange when dried. Strong flavor that smells like nutmeg. Mace can be sued on desserts, spice cakes, custards, cookies, carrots, broccoli, cauliflower, Brussels sprouts, creamed soups and stews.

**Marjoram-herb (fresh sprigs, leaves-dried or ground)** It is an oval inch long pal green leaf. Marjoram is a member of the mint and oregano family. It is aromatic, but slightly bitter. Marjoram is used in soups, stews, marinades, on fish, meats, poultry, sausage, stuffing and vegetables. Marjoram will hold its fragrance when dried better than most herbs. It is especially good in beef stew used in Mediterranean and Middle Easter foods. Marjoram tea aids digestion (even colic in children) and increases sweating. Used as a steam inhalant, it will help clear the sinuses.

**Mint-herb (leaves or flakes)** There are over 25 varieties of mint, however the most popular are Peppermint and Spearmint. It has a strong, sweet flavor with a cool after taste. It is very aromatic. Mint is used in beverages, jello, ice cream, teas (hot and cold) desserts, lamb, sauces, soups and stews.

**Mustard Seed-spice (whole or ground)** Small seeds of the mustard plant. They are white or yellow or light brown seeds. Mustard seeds are hot and pungent, a spicy rustic taste. The brown seeds are stronger. They are used in meats, pickling, relishes, sauces, gravies, soup, and stews.

**Nutmeg-spice (whole or ground)** Gray-brown oval seed from the nutmeg tree. It has a nutty warm, spicy, sweet taste. Mace is obtained from the membrane of the seeds. Can be sued in beverages, cakes, cookies, sauces, sweet potatoes and soups and stews and vegetables. I really like it on Brussels sprouts. It is also tasty in eggnog, mulled wine, and cider.

**Oregano-herb ( fresh leaves or crumbled dried)** It is a member of the mint family and related to thyme and marjoram. The flavor is strong and aromatic. It is widely used in Greek, Spanish and Italian cuisine. Together with basil, it is associated with many Italians dishes and is also found on most pizzas, spaghetti sauces, and marinara sauces. It also complements beef or lamp stews, gravies, salads, soups and even tomato juice. It is a very popular herb.

**Paprika-spice (ground)** It is ground from the dried Capsico (bell pepper). It is dried, red pepper ground into a powder. It has a slightly bitter flavor, but can range from sweet to hot. It is used in fish, poultry, salad (especially potato salad) , soups, stews. Partially used in Hungarian goulash. It is also used as a decoration as color in certain food selection.

**Parsley-herb (fresh sprigs or crumbled dried)** Two of the most popular types of parsley are curly leaf and Italian flat leaf parsley. Slightly peppery in flavor. It is used as a garnish and in soups, stews, sauces, poultry, fish, tomatoes and many vegetables as well as in herb mixes. It is one of the most popular and widely used herbs.

**Pepper (peppercorn)-spice (whole, ground or cracked)** Berries are from the pepper plant and grown in a grape-like cluster. There are black, white, and green peppercorns that are used. It has a peppery, hot taste. It can be used on most everything to enhance the flavor.

**Poppy Seeds-spice (whole)** It is a very small round blue-gray seed. It has a crunchy texture with a nutty flavor. It is used in baking breads, cakes, muffins and pastries, salad dressings, vegetables, soups, and sauces. Have you every had a roll that had poppy seeds on it? Yum.

**Rosemary-herb (fresh sprigs or whole dried)** It is a silver-green needle shaped leaf and is a member of the mint family. It is very aromatic with a faint lemony pine scent. It is used in soups and stews, casseroles, salads, stuffing and meat, fish and chicken dishes.

**Saffron-spice (whole threads or powdered)** Dried yellow-orange threads from the saffron crocus plant .When used or added to food, it changes to a bright yellow color. Can be steeped in hot liquid. It is a very pungent and aromatic spice. It is very expensive, so use sparingly. Saffron is used in rice and many rice dishes, sauces, soups and strews, in Spanish recipes, curries and bouillabaisse.

**Sage-herb (fresh sprigs, dried, whole leaves and crumbled, or ground)** It is a narrow oval grey green slightly furry leaf. They really are quite attractive in appearance. Slightly musty, minty taste, but a powerful herb, use in moderation. It is used in chicken, duck, goose, sausage, soups, stews, and the best is used in stuffing for the holidays.

**Savory-herb (fresh springs and crumbled dried)** There are two types of savory—winter and summer. The summer savor is slightly milder, but both have a strong flavor and, therefore, use sparingly. They are in the mint family and blend well with mint and thyme. Savory has a minty, aromatic, slightly pungent fragrance. It is used in soups, stews, meat, fish, stuffing and some bean dishes. It is also used in a fine herb mixture.

**Sesame Seed-spice (dried whole seeds)** It is a tiny, flat seed that is pale grayish or ivory (most commonly used) or brown, red, black. Sesame seeds are nutty, slightly sweet flavor. It is used in breads, cakes, cookies, dips, salads, dressing, soups, seafood, and chicken. Do you know what is on the hamburger roller that you have eaten? The hamburger roller is garnished with Sesame Seeds. It adds a crunch to many Asian dishes. It is 'Tahini', which is a sesame seed paste. Sesame seeds are great on broccoli with a little lemon juice.

**Tarragon-herb (leave whole or crunched)** Tarragon is a narrow, pointed dark green leaf. It has a mild licorice flavor (like anise). It is used on eggs, meat, fish and chicken, pickling, salads, sauces, in fine herb blends, soups and stews.

**Thyme-herb (leaves or ground)** Garden thyme (most common) is a bush with gray-green leaves. It is in the mint family. A pungent, minty tea-like flavor. It is one of my most used and favorite herb along with basil. Used in soups, stews, stuffing, salads, vegetables and on meat, fish. It is also used in fine herb blends. Fresh thyme can be stored in the refrigerator between paper towels. It should be added near the end of the heating process to keep the flavor strong.

**Turmeric-spice (ground)** It is a bright yellow-orange root of a tropical plant, which is related to ginger root. It can be used as a flavor or a coloring for food. It has a warm, peppery taste. Use with care as it will stain. It is pungent and somewhat bitter. It is used in some curries, American style mustard and some Indian recipes and stews. Keep in a tightly sealed container.

Compiled from www.yankeeharvest.com/spices, www.wikipedia.org , www.penzeys.com and www.wisegeek.com

# Dried to Fresh Herbs

When substituting dried herbs for fresh herbs the ratio is 1:3.

1 teaspoon to 3 teaspoons (3 teaspoons = 1 Tablespoon)

Use 1 teaspoon of dried herbs to 3 teaspoons or 1 Tablespoon of fresh herbs

## Conversion Changes for Tablespoons to Cups

| | | |
|---|---|---|
| 4 Tablespoons | = | ¼ cup |
| 8 Tablespoons | = | ½ cup |
| 12 Tablespoons | = | ¾ cup |
| 16 Tablespoons | = | 1 cup |
| 24 Tablespoons | = | 1 ½ cup |
| 32 Tablespoons | = | 2 cups |

Rosemary ©Connie Hope

Thyme © Connie Hope

Marjoram © Connie Hope

*Nothing is written in stone. Here are some other herbs that can be used or substituted in this mixture.

1 teaspoon dried basil
Or
½ teaspoon fennel seeds
Or
2 Tablespoons oregano
Or
1 teaspoon tarragon
Or
1 Tablespoon chervil

My favorite in this mixture is the lavender buds which add so much flavor.
You can also buy a container in most supermarkets or specialty stores with a variety of different dried herbs that they call Herbes de Provence.
Choose the one you like best.

*Wikipedia on the Internet

# Appendix

## Herbs

**Herbs de Provence** is a mixture of herbs typically of Provence, France. The standard mix contains savory, thyme, rosemary, fennel and marjoram. Lavender was not used in the original mix, but has been added over the years. This was because the tourist saw lavender fields as an example of the Provence region. This was a nice addition to the herb mix. Other possibilities are basil chervil, or tarragon. The mixture is used to flavor grilled fish, chicken, and meats, as well as vegetables, stews and soups. It is good in an olive oil mix for use with bread to dunk or used to coat the outside of chicken. It is very versatile.*

Herbes de Provence © Connie Hope

### Herbes de Provence

5 Tablespoons dried thyme
3 Tablespoons dried savory
2 Tablespoons dried marjoram
5 Tablespoons dried rosemary
1 ½ Tablespoons dried lavender buds

Use a fork to mix ingredients together in a small glass bowl.
Store in an airtight container.
Makes about 1 cup.

# Appendix

## How to Dry Herbs

The most important information to learn about drying herbs is the time of day. Herbs should be picked before the flowers develop, and harvested on a warm, dry morning after the dew has evaporated. This way the leaves will not be damp and mildew will not form.

Discard any damaged leaves. Strip large herbed leaves such as sage or mint from the stalk. However, small feathery leaves such as dill or fennel should be left on the stalk until drying is complete.

For beginners, it is best to start with tarragon, sage, bay, mint, lavender, and rosemary. I have explained four methods of drying so that you understand what you can do. Being the modern lady that I am, I prefer the microwave drying as it is less time consuming and controllable.

There are many methods to dry leaves. Choose the one that works best for you.

## Hanging Dry-use a well ventilated place out of direct sunlight

Tie springs or branches into small bunches and hang them up to dry. The leaves should be downward. Wrap loosely in muslin or a thin paper bag. This will keep out dampness and catch any falling leaves. You should allow between seven (7) to ten (10) days to dry. If the leaves are crispy, they should be completely dry.

## Rack Drying

If you space out individual sprigs or leaves of herbs on a rack, you can speed up the drying time. To create a drying rack, use a wooden frame and stretch out muslin, cheesecloth or netting. Find an airy, out of direct sunlight spot. Turn the leaves frequently to ensure even drying.

## Oven Drying

Space out leaves on a muslin-covered tray in an oven set at the lowest possible temperature. Leave the door ajar to allow the moisture to escape. Turn the leaves after 30 minutes to ensure even drying. After one hour they will be sufficiently dried. Turn the oven off, and leave in the oven until cooled.

# Microwave Drying

The microwave works well when drying small quantities of herbs. Separate the leaves from the stems, Place a single layer of leaves on a paper towel on a microwave-safe plate or platter. Place another paper towel on top. Microwave for 1 minute on high. Check after 30 seconds. Make sure that the leaves don't smell as they can burn. Continue heating at 15 second intervals and check for herbs to be fully dry.

Now that you have dried the herbs, what do you do with them?

Crumble the dried herbs with your fingers. Discard the center hard leafstalk or mid ribs. Store in a small airtight containers. Store in a dark place, so the herbs don't lose their color.

Dried herbs are used in cooking foods, but remember that drying concentrates the flavors, so you don't need to use as much in a recipe. If a recipe states 1 Tablespoon of fresh herbs, use only 1 teaspoon of dried herbs.

Good luck and have fun drying herbs.

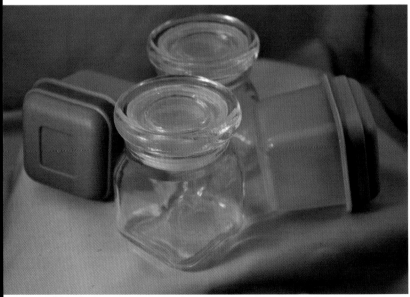

www.wikipedia.org , www.tasteofhome.com , and www.wikihow.com .

# Appendix

## Containers of broth used in cooking

One of the tricks I use is a base for chicken, beef, vegetables and mushrooms. You can use these for stock, soups, stews, gravies and just about anything that needs a sauce. Here are several that I have found work great.

Organic **Better than Bouillon** ® at www.superiortouch.com Superior Quality Foods, Ontario, CA 91761
It comes in Chicken, Mushroom, Beef and Vegetable and others. It is a paste consistency and can be put in water and heated. You use one teaspoon of the base and one cup of boiling water. I use it for my stock or broth for soups, add to stews or even make gravy with it.

**Knorr Bouillon** ® cubes. They come in tomato, vegetable, beef and chicken. I use 1 to 2 cups of boiling water. This can be used in soups, for poaching fish, for pasta, and most dishes that you use broth with.

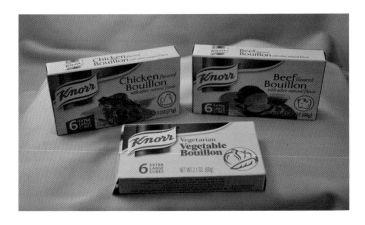

**McCormick** ® also makes a good chicken base. It comes in a 16 oz jar and goes a long way. I make broth out of this also.

**Green Chiles** are not always easy to find. I usually keep several jars in my cupboard. Ortega packages them as does Old El Paso. Ortega is at www.ortega.com where you can find some recipes and other bits of information. Old El Paso is at www.bettycrocker.com/oldelpaso

# Appendix

## Better than Bouillon

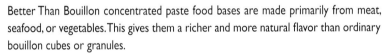

Better Than Bouillon concentrated paste food bases are made primarily from meat, seafood, or vegetables. This gives them a richer and more natural flavor than ordinary bouillon cubes or granules.

Better than Bouillon Concentrated Stocks are made from meat (or vegetables). This gives them a richer, more robust flavor than ordinary bouillons or soup bases. The Chicken tastes like Chicken because it IS Chicken; the beef tastes like beef because it IS beef. No Fat, Lower Sodium: Better Than Bouillon Concentrated Stocks are fat free and have 1/3 less salt than ordinary bouillons. Most supermarkets have them in 8 oz containers, but Costco has the 16 oz. This is the one I use a lot.

The different kinds are Beef Base, Chicken Base, Chili Base, Clam Base, Fish Base, Ham Base, Lobster Base, Mushroom Base, Turkey Base and Vegetable Base.

# Appendix

## Stir in Paste by Gourmet Garden

Gourmet Garden makes tubes of herbs that you can stir in sauces, soups, stews and many other dishes you make. They are the freshest of herbs that are stored in your refrigerator for up to three (3) months. I think they are great for cooking anything; they add excellent flavors to your dishes.

I'm always looking for an easier way to cook and these tubes certainly fit that idea. They are flavorful and simple to use. Check them out at your supermarket. I find them at my market in the fresh vegetable refrigerated section near the mushroom and celery. You may have to ask an attendant where they are located in your market. My favorite is the Lemongrass. It just adds so much flavor to soups and stews.

They also make a 'Lightly Dried' herb container. It is the closest thing to fresh.

Here is a list of the herbs they have in tubes as paste:

| | |
|---|---|
| Basil | Chives |
| Chili pepper | Fennel |
| Cilantro | Rosemary |
| Dill | Marjoram |
| Italian Herbs | Sage |
| Garlic | Mint |
| Chunky garlic | Savory |
| Ginger | Thyme |
| Lemongrass | Tarragon |
| Oregano | Sorrel |
| Parsley | Watercress |
| Thai Seasoning | |

# Appendix

## Basil Pesto

2 cups fresh basil leaves, packed firmly
1/3 cup pine nuts, walnuts, pecans, or whatever
3 medium sized cloves of garlic minced (If you really like
    Garlic, add more to your taste.)
½ cup extra virgin olive oil
½ cup, freshly grated cheese (Parmesan or Romano or
    whatever)
Salt and fresh ground pepper (I use a lime pepper made by
  Jane's Krazy Mixed-Up Seasonings®

Combine basil and nuts in a food processor and pulse.
Add garlic and pulse.
Slowly add the olive oil in a steady stream.
Scrape sides and pulse again.
Add the cheese if you are not going to freeze the pesto.
Salt and fresh ground pepper to taste.
If you are freezing, put into ice cube trays or in an airtight
    container and refrigerate.

Pesto can be served on many things, so use your
    imagination.

### Here are just a few ideas:

• On pizza in place of or in addition to the red sauce.
• Add to an Alfredo sauce.
• Stir into mashed potatoes.
• Stir into risotto.
• Put a dollop on soup.
• Combine with mayonnaise on sandwich or toppings.
• Add to scrambled eggs or fold into omelets.

During the summer my basil flourishes and I can't use it up fast enough. What to do? Well, I make Basil Pesto.

Serve with:
Soups
Stews
Pasta
Baked potatoes
Appetizers with toast
Over fish or chicken

It is a recipe that you can change to your taste. Most pesto calls for parmesan cheese, but if you like romano better, then substitute.

I freeze my pesto. Omit the cheese until you serve it. I put it in ice cube trays, let it freeze, then pop it out into a freezer bag. It will store for several months.

My favorite is 'pesto on pasta.' I pop out 2-3 ice cubes of pesto and put them in a pot. I use a little white wine and a little water and heat. Make any type of pasta (I like bow ties best.) and put your pesto on top. Add your cheese. Viola!

Basil Pesto © Connie Hope

All the ingredients are finely chopped:

1 cup green olives
1 cup kalamata olives
½ cup marinated
    artichokes
1/3 cup red bell peppers
3 green onions,
1 clove garlic, minced
¼ cup celery
2 Tablespoons parsley
2 teaspoons dried oregano
3 Tablespoons red wine
    vinegar
¾ cup olive oil

# Appendix

## Olive Muffalata

The Muffalata is a New Orleans sandwich with cured meats, cheese and a tangy olive salad piled on an Italian loaf of bread called Muffalata. The olive salad is like a spread.

This is a famous blend of ripe, juicy olives and succulent garden vegetables mixed together with soybean oil. It can be added to meats, stews, and just about anything. You have to taste it to believe the rich flavor and taste.

It consists of ripe olives, cauliflower, peppers, celery, carrots, spices, and soybean oil all chopped up together in a jar. If you have a ho hum dinner, just add a few Tablespoons of Olive Muffalata and it will bring new taste to your meal.

Here is a photo of the what it looks like, but you need to try it to get the full effect. I get it at Costco, but most specialty stores would have it. Maybe even your supermarket.

Here is one recipe for Mufalata, if you wanted to try and make it yourself. There are many different recipes for it. You can also buy it premade at the supermarket.

Muffalata © Connie Hope

# Cooking Green in Your Kitchen 101

What does it mean to be cooking green in your kitchen? Let's take a closer look at what you can do in your own kitchen to help the environment. If we each do a little, a lot can be accomplished.

### 1. Recycle your food scraps

You can turn your coffee grounds, apple peels, banana peels, egg shells into rich compost for your garden, lawn and any houseplants just by keeping a small container (ie. bucket, crock) to collect waste scrapes in your kitchen. Have a backyard compost container to put the kitchen collection in. They are many different outdoor and indoor safe compost system. Check them out at Home Depot, Lowes, Ace hardware or Google them. There are two website to visit epa.org and earth911. org to start.

### 2. Recycle your glass, paper, plastic and metal.

Set up a bin and put these items in it to go out for waste recycling. Again, check the internet for suggestions on recycling in your town or county.

### 3. Heat only what you will use.

A small appliance such as a toaster oven or microwave is more energy efficient than a large oven. These small appliances are great for smaller portions. A 2-4 cup coffee pot uses less energy and water than a 12 cup coffee pot. An electric kettle for boiling water uses less power than heating water on the stove.

### 4. Glass is back!

I know storing leftovers in plastic containers is what we have always done, then discard them after several uses. That is a lot of plastic in our environment. Try the old fashion glass or stainless steel containers. They can be cleaned and reused over and over. Make an effort to do this.

### 5. How are 'veggie' wrappings?

Be aware of how your "veggies" are sold. Better to buy broccoli heads than broccoli in a styrofoam tray with plastic shrink wrap. The tray is hard to get rid of and recycle. Better to buy without these storage containers.

# Index

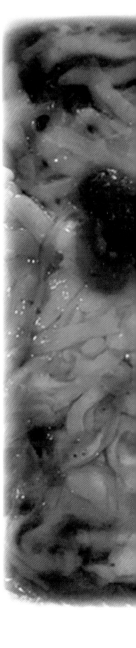

# About the Author

Writing has always been my passion. When I was ten years old, I won first prize in a Patriotism Contest sponsored by the Children of the American Revolution. I said to my mother, "I want to be a writer." She replied "Find a profession that will pay some money." I wrote articles for the school newspaper, the local newspaper and magazines, but it wasn't until I moved to Florida a decade ago that I decided it was now my time to write books.

I spent a year and a half creating my first cookbook, *"In Addition…to the Entrée"* about the important side dishes which compliments main dish. It is a personal guide to help the busy working person as well as anyone else to decide what to serve as a side dish for the meal. The book has one hundred and sixty pages, over two hundred color photos, and is divided into fourteen sections with an extensive index.

Next I started working on my novel, *"The Bonnie Neuk Tea Room: Friends and Uninvited Guests (Ghosts)"*. Victoria Storm is facing a divorce and wants to do something different with the rest of her life. But what? She receives a cell phone call from someone who suggests she opens a tea room as her grandmother did in her hometown of Metuchen, New Jersey. And who was that who called?

Victoria buys an old house, renovates it into a tea room and eventually has numerous encounters with uninvited guests, or are they ghosts?

My second cookbook, *"Soups and Stews...Comfort by the Spoonful"* is a labor of pure love. Making soups and stews is something I enjoy doing. I make soup at least once a week, regardless of the weather. And in Florida it can definitely be hot. The book has 220 pages with over 200 colored photos of soups and stews. I hope you enjoy it!

Please check out www.cookingbyconnie.com and thebonnieneuktearoom. com for more information, ordering, pricing, and photos. *In Addition...to the Entree* is $15.00, Soups and Stews...*Comfort by the Spoonful* is $20.00, and *The Bonnie Neuk Tea Room: Friends and Uninvited Guests (Ghosts)* is $10.00, plus $5.00 postage each, if you want one mailed.

You can purchase any of these books through me or at The Bonnie Neuk website, www.bonnieneuktearoom.com My novel can also be purchased through Createspace at www.Createspace.com/4775503 or on Amazon.com Amazon.com The cookbooks are at my house. Call 215-527-1217 or email me at conniehope@comcast.net to order them. I will sign and mail it to you.

Enjoy!

Connie Hope